I
CURED
MY
ARTHRITIS
YOU CAN TOO

By

Margie Garrison

Published by
MARGIE GARRISON

I CURED MY ARTHRITIS
YOU CAN TOO

By

MARGIE GARRISON

Published by **Margie Garrison**

Margie Garrison
P.O. Box 684
Wyandotte, MI 48192

Library of Congress Catalog Card Number 80-70018
ISBN #0-912835-00-1

1st Printing January, 1981
2nd Printing August, 1981
3rd Printing April, 1982
4th Printing July, 1982
5th Printing September, 1982
6th Printing September, 1983
Revised Printing September, 1984
9th Printing, 1988
10th Printing May, 1989
11th Printing November, 1989
12th Printing April, 1990
13th Printing June, 1990

I dedicate this book to my loving husband, who would have done anything he could to free me from pain ..... He showed love, compassion and understanding during the years of coping with the problems caused by my pain. I am grateful for his full cooperation when I set out on this — to me — unknown path to a pain-free life. Without the kind of help and encouragement he provided, the journey would have been almost impossible. I would have done it, but, oh, how hard it would have been.

To my children, who always gave me their total love and caring and the feeling that, for them, I was a very important person ..... what I wanted ..... they wanted for me. My happiness is their happiness.

My family gave me love instead of indifference. Sympathy instead of disinterest. Encouragement instead of criticism. Praise for each small victory instead of non-interest.

I will always be grateful.

CONTENTS

FOREWORD

Margie Garrison is "A NEW BREED OF LAYMAN." The layman equivalent of Dr. Alan H. Nittler's, "A NEW BREED OF DOCTOR." Indeed, Margie and the hoard of the new breed of layman are a challenge to the Medical Establishment. When doctors (specialists of arthritis) condemned her existence to a lifelong suffering of pain and increasing doses of harmful and addictive drugs, saying, "Bear with it. . . . . . there is no cure for arthritis . . . . . you will be in a wheelchair within five years," Margie did not accept their verdict. She figured out all by herself, "There *is* a cause for arthritis and if there is a cause, then there must be a remedy . . . . if the doctors did not know anything about it, it did not mean there was no remedy" . . . . . And with this optimistic rational, she charged into the pathway of "Search for Truth."

Margie tells us the story of her "Painful Odyssey through the Medic-World," and her pleasant adventures into the world of knowledge of nutrition and optimum health. Needless to say, she cured her arthritis . . . . . "THE INCURABLE DISEASE." The Medical Establishment will call this "spontaneous remission," yet Margie can turn her arthritis on and off to the tune of a melody. She has learned which foods trigger her arthritic pains and aches.

Six months ago, when Margie first came to my office for Nutrition Consultation, her main concern was her obesity, at 260 pounds for her 5 ft., 5½ inches. After two hours of questioning, I realized that she did not consider a major problem the fact that she still had about 20% of her arthritic pains and aches. For her having suffered constant pain for almost forty years, having cured herself of 80% of her pains was such a heavenly blessing she could bear slight aches and ignore them. When I mentioned to her the fact that I could not put her on any weight reduction program until her aches were cured 100% and until she felt super-duper, her eyes sparkled with incredulous amazement and pleasure. Apparently, being free of pain 100% of the time had been to her such a "Sweet and unattainable dream" that she embarked on her new program with the enthusiasm of a pioneer.

At the time of writing this book, she made a confession that when she first came to my office, she thought nutritionists were mainly concerned with such things as dieting, weight loss, special diets for diabetes. The conventional "Dietetics" approach to nutrition. She thought . . . . . putting it in her words . . . . . "I was afraid to tell you; I thought you would pooh-pooh me for telling you I had cured my arthritis by eliminating certain foods from my diet . . . . . arthritis is supposed to be an incurable disease."

Naturally, what Margie discovered was that I not only believed in her claims, but encouraged her to complete her self-cure.

I can substantiate her claims that she is 100% free of pain. Free of swelling. Although pain is a subjective feeling, and only a "Symptom" and not a "sign" for the skeptical doctor to substantiate or quantify it, pain has a unique characteristic to register itself on the face of the bearer.

Margie has become her perky, cheerful self and, despite her busy schedule of working in the family business and extensive traveling, managed to write her book. She has two important messages in her book. To the layman, her message says, "Annie, get your gun" and start singing "Anything you can do, I can do better." Put your body in your hands and use the right bullets. Use nutrition, exercise, relaxation and aim at your health, your "optimum health." With some trial and error, you, too, will learn to aim correctly.

To the doctors, her message simply says, "Mirror,

mirror on the wall, who is the knowledgeable of them all?" It is time that doctors and medical students assess the type and amount of knowledge they are receiving from "The Establishment." Are they getting their dollar's worth? Going to medical school is a very expensive investment and if they are being short-changed and because of this their patients will abandon them and seek self-cure, within the next few decades, a doctor may be an obsolete figure in our society, not because there will not be sick people, but because sick people, untrustful of their doctor's knowledge and abilities, will seek help elsewhere than the doctor's offices.

Sick people who become disenchanted with their doctors do not necessarily find another doctor who is knowledgeable in Preventive Medicine, since although the ranks of this new breed of doctors are increasing, it is still difficult for the average person to locate one in his/her neighborhood. What the sick people have easy access to are: popular books, health food stores, lay nutritionists and various non-conventional outlets. By trial and error, by reading, the determined person does improve his/her health to a degree that most describe as, "I can not describe how miserable I was and how much money, time I wasted going from one doctor to another. If the cure for my problem was such a simple thing as changing my eating habits and a few vitamins and minerals, how come all these doctors do not know anything about it? I feel like trying to educate doctors on nutrition. It is a blessing I have come so far and I consider this a great improvement."

What the sick person has access to does not necessarily guarantee what he/she really needs. This is the case of many clients who walk into my office for Nutrition Consultation. Invariably, while their nutrition is along the lines of healthful eating and they have a bagful of bottles to show me what supplements they have tried, I find several major gaps and sometimes major errors in their haphazard trial and error. I do not condemn the lay-nutritionists, nor the efforts of the patients for self-cure. On the contrary, any patient who comes to my office with such a background gets a friendly pat on the back.

The point I want to raise is for the doctors. If there were doctors who were trained in the gold mine of "Nutrition Therapy," then patients would not seek the lay and the non-conventional help. Americans do depend upon their doctors for their health just as they depend upon their cars for transportation. It is part of the American way of life.

There is no such thing as an "INCURABLE DISEASE." All diseases are curable if we only knew and applied the right measures. For all diseases are preventable by maintaining optimum health through orthomolecular nutrition and orthomolecular environment.

Correct molecular environment inside and outside of our bodies, guarantees not only a disease-free body, but optimum health.

It is a pleasure to present to you Margie Garrison . . . . "THE FIRST SELF-CURE SPECIALIST."

Felor Jourdikian, Ph.D.

*"TODAY IS THE FIRST
DAY OF THE REST OF
YOUR LIFE"*

Chapter I
WHY I WROTE THIS BOOK

From the age of eleven to the age of fifty-two in 1978, I had suffered from almost constant pain. The memory of the first night is as clear today as if it was yesterday. The pain was unbearable.

My mother, an aunt, an uncle, and several cousins and I went to an amusement park in Detroit, Michigan, called Bob-Lo Island. I slipped while getting into a ride. It hurt at the time, but, like any eleven-year-old, I ignored it and had a good time the rest of the night. The amusement park is on an island, so one takes a long boat ride to get there. It was on the return ride that my knees began to ache. More accurately, behind my knees. It got worse and worse. I told my mother, but she said it was probably because I was tired. It was a lovely, moonlit night and everyone around me was singing and being happy, but I cried all the way home.

From that time on, every night became a battle. Days were all right, but as soon as I would settle down to read or sit for any period of time, my knees would hurt. After about three years of this, my mother said she thought it was growing pains, and that was that. So I accepted that.

I was very active in High School. Even though at times my legs hurt, I was determined not to let it interfere with my life. When night came, it was always painful. I just could not sit down. It seemed I spent my life wiggling. I seemed to be the only one in my group that ever had that kind of pain. I felt isolated and alone and learned very early that no one is interested in your aches and pains, so I kept it to myself.

My mother's best friend was married to a Chiropractor and he felt he could help me. So, at the age of fifteen, I started on what proved to be a two-year program of going to him twice a week. I had adjustments on my back. He said my spine was out of place. There was some relief, but it never lasted. Dr. T.D. was very concerned about me. His feelings were that the pain stemmed from my lower back. However, at the end of two years, he felt he could not help me any more. Both my mother and I were very disappointed.

It was in High School that I started taking aspirin. Also, the beginning of my questions as to just what was my pain. My Gym teacher said I should just stand up straight. I spent much time lying down on the gym floor trying to flatten the small of my back to the floor. She was always able to slip her hand between my back and the floor, so she kept after me to do it over and over. I could not do it. I found out twenty-five years later, when I went to a back specialist, that I had a congenital spinal problem. It seems that the last vertebra at the base of my spine never developed. Dr. T.D. expressed sympathy, but said there was no help for that problem.

The first serious trips from one doctor to another started when I was twenty-five. My mother and I both felt we should go back to her friend the chiropractor. In the almost ten years since I had my last adjustment, maybe new things had come to light. I had one, and sometimes two, adjustments a week for about ten months. I remember having to lie down on the car seat during the trip there and back because I just could not sit up straight for any length of time. There was

no apparent change, so I stopped.

At the age of twenty-seven, after the birth of my third child, I went to the Arthritis Foundation and was given several names of doctors who specialized in arthritis in Grand Rapids, Michigan. Dr. D. made tests and told me it was Osteo-Arthritis. He recommended aspirin as the  only relief available. I asked if there was something he could do? He said no. Take aspirin and bear with it. He said there was no cure, but the Arthritis Foundation was looking for a cure.

At the age of twenty-eight, I went through the same procedure. Calling the Arthritis Foundation, getting several names of doctors specializing in arthritis, making an appointment and seeing Dr. G. He confirmed what Dr. D. had said. But he sprayed my back and knees with some medication out of a spray can. It numbed the skin and felt wonderful, but only lasted a few hours, and could only be done in the doctor's office. So, it was not only impractical, but inconvenient.

In 1955, at the age of twenty-nine, and two months after the birth of my fourth child, my daughter Susan, Dr. J. put me in a hospital for a week. I had multiple tests, including a spinal tap. The pain from this was very severe. I had to stay bent over at a certain angle and not move while they put this long needle into my spine. I do not know if it was my fault or theirs, but it took them several tries and I ended up in tears.

Dr. J. diagnosed Osteo-Arthritis and a low-back problem. Dr. J. was represented to me as the best man in Michigan, at that time. I told him the pain was now in my wrists and ankles. The pain would move around from place to place. He told me to go home and make the best of it because within five years I would be in a wheelchair. I was shocked. Not only at what he said, but how he said it. So off-handedly. I felt he had absolutely no compassion for me — no feeling that he would help me bear the gradual decline. Just "GO HOME AND BEAR IT."

I went home. I bore with it, but I did not accept his verdict. I am and always have been a positive thinker. I did not get depressed. I had a long talk with myself and said, "Since the authorities do not know anything about arthritis, he is probably wrong and I will not let it stop me." In the year 1980, at the age of fifty-three, I am still not in a wheelchair.

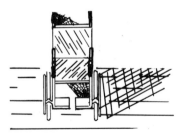

I have always worked. From the age of sixteen, first as a waitress, then at the age of twenty-one, as a Direct Sales lady selling to women by appointment in their homes. I would work during the school months and stay at home during the summer when I would enjoy my children and spend as much time as I could in bed resting my back.

I was blessed with wonderful children. From the birth of Tom, the oldest, I adjusted to the limitations of my pains, caused by my arthritis problems. I learned the right way for me to bend over to diaper my babies. Tom learned that momma could not pick him up as he would like. He would make his way into my lap by himself. He learned that toys gotten out by him were put away by him, because he knew I could not bend over. When he was 2½, Mike was born. Tom already was accustomed to doing what he could for me. He was very helpful. He also set an example for Mike. When Mike was 2, Charles was born. I now had three of the best children you could ask for. Charles had a harder time understanding that momma was not there to answer his every beck and call, but he learned. I remember one day when Tom was about six. I hurt extra bad and my patience was gone. I was screaming at the three boys for nothing in particular. They were looking at me, as if to say, "Gee, whiz, we're not doing anything." Then Tom took both Mike and Chuck by the hand and said, "Come on, let's us kids get out of here."

When Chuck was 2, I had my fourth and last child. It was a darling little girl, Susan. By then, the boys were doing dishes, making their own beds, putting away their dirty clothes, lifting for me when I needed it. They knew that if anything fell on the floor, they were to pick it up — whether it was toys, food, or whatever I dropped. I do not want to make them out as angels. They were not angels. But they were so attuned to the problem that their momma had that it was second nature to them to help. We did everything together, went places, and really enjoyed ourselves.

The boys were so thankful for a sister because, now, they could see an end to doing dishes and dusting. It is still a surprise to me how much children observe and are able to accustom themselves to.

One night, when Susan was about 4, we had my cousins and their five children over for the evening. The kids were about the same ages and had a great time. When their mother said it was time to go, her kids dropped what they were playing with and started getting ready to go. My

children really let them know that in this house, the children who got the toys out were the ones to put them away. Without any prompting from me, they made sure every toy was put away before they let them put on their coats and leave.

I disciplined my children with a slipper because it had just the right softness and was pliant. They knew that when I said they were going to be spanked, it meant that they were to get the slipper and come to me. I did not go to them.

One day, a girl friend, Eleanor, was visiting with her six-year-old boy, who was Susan's age. He was extremely naughty and I was wondering when Eleanor would stop him. She finally started screaming at him to stop, then, when that did not work, she started chasing him all over the yard, yelling, "When I catch you, you're going to get it!!" My kids just stood there looking, and then Mike said, "Boy, we could never get away with that."

When I was thirty-one, I repeated the quest for help!! I should have been discouraged by then with the Arthritis Foundation and their recommendations. But it was the only game in town. And my optimism said, "Maybe, now, they know more." So the new specialist, Dr. M., said, "Oh, you need a back brace and that will stop the pain." The doctor was very self-assured. Seemed to have no doubt about his verdict. He examined me with great condescension and said, "You do not have arthritis!! You just need this brace!!" I wore the steel brace for three months. It was hot that summer and I thought I would melt. The brace went from the top of my thighs to four inches above my waist. After three months of no relief, I threw it away.

More aspirin. Sometimes even my toes would hurt. Nights still the worst time. It got so I was taking as many as 26 aspirins a day. My ears would ring so much and so loudly I could not sleep because of the noise.

I guess after the last doctor I became resigned. I did not see another doctor until I was 35. I had moved to Flint, Michigan, and again called the Arthritis Foundation. Getting the names of several specialists, I chose Dr. P., made an appointment, and waited. He did not examine me physically, just took my written record, and gave me two treatments of cortisone about a week apart. He then gave me several gold treatments. The cortisone made me puffy, but neither treatment helped me, so I stopped.

So, back to aspirin. From this time until I got on Codeine, I was taking at least 15 aspirin and usually 26 a day. Dr. P., whom I went to see again after about six months, prescribed Codeine. I used this for about two years, and when I asked Dr. P. for something stronger, he stopped m prescription for Codeine. I was shaken. Codeine was not perfect, but I did get some relief from pain. But he said, "No more because I would become addicted." So, back to aspirin.

When I was thirty-seven, I chose another specialist from the Foundation's list. Dr. T. He made some tests, told me, with sort of a sneer, "Well, you do not have arthritis; you have a low threshold for pain!!" Well!!! After having suffered for years and done rather well in bearing it, he had the nerve to tell me that I was a cry baby. To illustrate why this upset me, let me digress for a moment and tell you a little story.

It had been about six years since the last time I had seen my father. I made a surprise visit one day. When he saw it was I at the door, he came roaring out and threw his arms around me and squeezed me. In doing this, the end of his cigarette pressed into my wrist. It burned me. Because he was so glad to see me and I did not want to make him feel remorse for hurting me, I just tightened up and did not say a word. To this day, I have a scar the size of the end of a cigarette on my left wrist and to the day of his death, he never knew what he did. So you can see why the doctor's statement made me feel badly.

This doctor said my left leg was shorter than my right leg and prescribed lifts put on my left shoe. He even gave me the name of a shoe man who would do it. Since I was the sufferer, and he was "THE AUTHORITY," I had it done. It cost me a lot of money and was unlovely, and it did not work. So, another try with the Foundation.

Dr. W. took my history and with well-meaning words, said, "Where did your last doctor come up with that idea your one leg was shorter? It is not; you have Osteo-Arthritis." But neither did this doctor offer me any help, except the time-honored: "There is nothing I can do; go home, accept it, take aspirin, and try to bear with it."

I must make clear here that at no time up to this point, after twenty-five years of seeing doctors, not one asked me what I ate. Since my weight was normal at 145 pounds for my 5 ft. 5½ inches, I assume they felt there was no need to go into what I ate.

I was now forty-two years old. Still in almost constant pain. A complete change in my life style had occurred. I no longer worked as a sales lady. My husband had his office attached to our house and had several girls work there besides his secretary. We got into the habit of having lots of donuts around. If any were left, I always seemed to eat them. I am sure it was the combination of staying home and eating more and more sweets that caused me to gain weight. I put on 55 pounds within one year. I now weighed 200 pounds. So I looked for a doctor who could help me lose weight.

I found a wonderful doctor who was vitally concerned with all his patients. Gave each of us the feeling that we were his only patient and he cared. I mentioned my arthritis to him, but he was not involved with treating that. He gave me a prescription for Darvon. He was only to treat me for weight. Started me on diuretics and hormone shots. I did not lose!!! In fact, by the time I was forty-four, I gained another 33 pounds. I was concerned, but Dr. T.Z. was so nice, I hated to ask him what was the reason I could not lose, and, instead, was gaining more. He advised me to eat all the meat, fish, cheese, vegetables and fruit I wanted, no bread, and the weight would go down by itself. It did not. The Darvon was relieving my pain and I was more free of pain than I had been since I was eleven. I was afraid to stop seeing the doctor for fear I could not get any more Darvon.

I always made sure I never went anywhere without at least two days' supply of Darvon, even if it were only to go to a show or to friends for an evening. Of course, gradually, I started taking just one more each day, and one more. Until I realized that my daily intake was 12 to 14 Darvon. And sometimes that was not enough. I told Dr. T.Z. and he did blood tests, said, so far, there was no damage from the Darvon, and that he would test me at least once a year. I knew I should never go to the heavier drugs, so I began to become concerned. Panic is more the word. The one side effect of all that Darvon was that I seemed to be in a daze most of the time. Not bad, just sort of off center.

During one visit, I again told Dr. T.Z. that my arthritis was getting worse and could he recommend someone. He gave me the name of Dr. P., but warned me that Dr. P only had office hours twice a week, and it might take several months to get an appointment. He was right. It took over two months to get an appointment, and then I had to wait from 9 a.m. to 3 p.m. to see him. The other patients sang his praises to me, so I did not mind the wait. After examining me, he agreed it was arthritis and a low-back problem. Told me to gradually work into some exercises he gave me, but not to do them if I felt heat at the point of pain. He also gave me a prescription for Darvon. I was never able to do the exercises because the heat never left the point of pain.

The next year, I asked my sister-in-law, who was a

nurse, to recommend someone. She did, but I must have a mental block because I can not remember his name. I do remember the hooked wires all over my chest and shoulders and head and how he sent electrical charges through them. It was rather uncomfortable, but did not hurt. He seemed to be totally involved with the test; he sure was not involved with me. He gave me no words of encouragement, just, "Yes, it is arthritis." No prescription, no help, just sent me home.

I then went to an acupuncture doctor in a nearby town. His office was crowded, but he was very efficient and the wait was never very long. I had a session twice a week for about a month. He would insert the needles in my knees, behind my knees and in my hips. It always relieved the pain for several hours, but the pain would then gradually return. It was also a forty minute drive one way and the cost plus the time made it impossible. I just could not take a whole day, twice a week, for the trip.

In the fall of 1978, when I had just turned fifty-two, I started reading nutrition books. I always considered I fed my family with good foods. We ate the typical diet. Cereals, fruits, vegetables cooked until they were nice and soft. Lots of beef. A meal was not a meal unless we had meat. I could never serve supper without a nice gooey dessert. Although I was strict on having fruit as a snack, we still had at least one sweet dessert a day. My children were all nice and slender. My husband was a little overweight, but nothing serious.

I read a book by Dr. Jack Goldstein, "Triumph Over Disease." (See chapter 9.) He had been to more doctors than I and had been sent home to die, but he cured himself through nutrition and fasting. I called. I was lucky, as we lived in the same city, and he gave me an appointment. He started me on an all raw diet of fruits, vegetables and nuts. He said this would take care of both my arthritis and my weight. I was faithful to it for a month, lost about fifteen pounds and felt much better. But, since I had no real knowledge as to why this type of food would help, I started gradually to add one thing here and there until I began to hurt a little more all over.

Started taking heavy doses of Darvon, again. The more I hurt, the more I ate, the more I ate, the more I hurt. I was desperate. I had been to all the doctors. I had taken as many drugs as I dared. I had suffered as much as I wanted to. I wanted relief. I wanted what other people seemed to have. Pain-free lives. I felt hopeless and helpless. As if I were alone in this jungle and could not see daylight. I had stopped seeing Dr. T.Z. Too ashamed to tell him I could not lose weight. I found a drugstore which would refill my prescription for Darvon. So I had my security blanket. I started letting my husband think I was taking less Darvon than I was. Not by outright lying, but by evasion. This gave me guilt feelings and I was beginning to hate the thought of him thinking I hurt extra badly, because then he would ask me how many Darvon I had taken already that day. I was becoming more and more tired. Spent more and more time lying down. I had been talking for years about riding the white water in the Grand Canyon with my husband and all the kids. That seemed to be getting farther and farther away. At times, it seemed as if that was going to be impossible to do.

Finally, in desperation, it hit home from all my reading of nutrition books that "NUTRITION WAS THE KEY." And with that realization, it was as if the sun had come out. As if the

prison door had just swung open. I felt hope and a great sense of jubilation. If nutrition was the answer, it followed that I was the one to control it. I was the one who put food into my mouth. And if this was so, I could see to it that I put in only the right foods.

Finally, July, 1979, when I was hurting a little more than I wanted to bear, I got the address of the place that Dr. Jack Goldstein had gone to. I called Dr. Goldstein and he was happy to give me the address. See Chapter 9 for address of the place.

I called them and made reservations for the following Sunday. I arrived there weighing 243 pounds, stayed on a total water fast for five days, lost fourteen pounds, but most important, for the first time, I was experiencing hours and hours of pain-free living without the use of drugs. I took no Darvon or aspirin the whole time I was there.

I broke my fast on the fifth day with an orange. The next day, I had salad and fruit and flew home and fasted at home for another seven days. The complete story is in another chapter. I read more on nutrition and started to see a pattern. All books seemed to agree on the treatment for arthritis. And the more I looked, the more books I found on how to cure arthritis. I was amazed. And angry. Some of the books had been in print for fifty years. Imagine, fifty years there had been written proof that arthritis could be cured and I had spent over forty years of pain and much money being told that I could not be helped. I became outraged and sad. The Arthritis Foundation says 30,000,000 people in this country, alone, have some form of arthritis. And I know they can be helped. I repeat, they can be helped. You can be helped if you really want to.

The more I thought about it, the more I was determined to write about my experiences and get the story to you who right now are in pain. You are walking the floor at night as I used to, you cannot sleep because of the pain right now. So stiff you can not bend over or get out of a chair without help. I almost cry sitting here typing these words and knowing that you can do what I did, and no one has told you how. I have more energy, do not hurt any more, and do not sleep as much. I wake refreshed instead of all dragged out.

You must remember, this is your pain, not your friends' or family's, that you are trying to get away from. You have a vested interest in getting rid of it.

The following chapters will be your guide. Only your guide. Sort of like a small path you can walk to find out more and more so you can hurt less and less.

I would like to write an open letter to all the doctors who treated me and to all the ones out there who are at a loss as to what to do for their arthritic patients.

Dear Doctors:

I appreciate the spirit in which most of you tried to help me. I am appreciative of all the time spent on me and others like me. I feel for you because of the lack of knowledge for the treatment of arthritis. I am no longer as angry as I was over the years of unnecessary suffering I endured because you did not have this knowledge. I realize now that the study of nutrition is a hard and complex one and that Medical Schools of today spend, at the most, three weeks, if they spend any time at all, on the study of Nutrition in relation to specific ailments. I truly believe that most doctors do an excellent job. I believe that at night, after a long, hard, frustrating day, they ask themselves, "Is there more I should know?" I know they do not have the time to study all the professional magazines and required studying they must do just to keep up. So I am not condemning the lack of success in treating me. I am just saying there is another way. There is hope for those with arthritis. The time is come for this knowledge to be put forth to all people suffering with arthritis.

It is twenty-eight years since you told me, "You will be in a wheelchair in five years."

I am not only not in a wheelchair, I walk two miles every day, do at least 20 minutes of exercises both morning and night. Have a very busy, active life. Have pain only when I chose to because I eat wrongly. I have not lost all my weight, yet, but that will come. As I study and continue to eat right, I believe strongly that I will not have a recurrence of my arthritis.

I thank you for your care. I hope you will accept from a lay person the history of "How I Cured My Arthritis."

If more people are made to become active in the cure of their own arthritis, you will have more time to devote to those whom you ARE helping.

Sincerely,

Margie Garrison

I have never felt better in my life. I feel stronger and younger and alive and I am looking forward to many happy, busy, pain-free years.

I CURED MY ARTHRITIS. YOU CAN, TOO.

> *"Whether it is down to Gehenna or up to the Throne — he travels the fastest who travels alone."*
>
> *Rudyard Kipling*

Chapter 2
HOW I CURED MY ARTHRITIS

On Sunday, July 29, 1979, I left the airport in Detroit for New York City. When I arrived, I got ground transportation for the three-hour drive to Pawling Health Manor. On the way, the driver stopped at a motel to pick up some passengers and I asked if there was time to get some water or pop. I wanted and needed to take one last Darvon. He laughed and said, "I hear that all the time from people going to the Manor. They feel it is like a last minute splurge. Usually, they buy candy."

It was 11:00 p.m. when I arrived, so they just very quietly showed me to my cottage. Since it was late, I did not get to see much, but I was put in an individual cottage with three beds. Mine was the middle one with women sleeping in the other two. I went quietly to bed and to sleep.

Monday, July 30. My first morning I slept till 8:00 a.m., when I felt someone taking my pulse. It was Dr. Gross. He gave me a little pep talk and welcomed me to the beginning of a new life. Also invited me to a lecture for the

new people on the program. It was to start at 10:00 a.m.

Before going to the lecture, I got acquainted with my roommates, Ellie and Pearl. More about them later.

The lecture was held in the living room of the mansion of Pawling Health Manor.

It is a large, stately building, circa 1890. Large rooms, high ceilings, and the very gracious feeling of elegant living. The color scheme was done in peach, on the walls and rugs, with accents of peach on the slip covers of the very comfortable furniture. There were about twenty new people at the lecture. Dr. Gross read some of the testimonial articles written about the Manor and its program. He explained why his program works.

We were to drink nothing but ice water. We could have as much as we liked, but were not to force drinking it. Only when thirsty. If we preferred, we could have it without ice. He told why the fast cures nothing. It just gives our very marvelous bodies the rest they need to heal themselves. That is why this treatment works for all illnesses. The fast cures nothing; it just lets our bodies do the work they are equipped to do.

After the lecture, I went back to my cottage and roommates. Ellie is from Toronto, and has been coming here once a year for a week of fasting to let her body have a rest and get her all set up for another year. She is a striking woman with a lovely tan she got the week previously in Florida. At the end of this week, she will be going back for another week in Florida with her husband.

Pearl is from Quebec and is a Grandmother, and this is her second time here. She comes to lose 10 pounds and relax, and also to let her body rest. She will be here for two weeks. She is a vegetarian. Has been for most of her life, raised her large family that way, and they are all very healthy.

I weighed in at 8:00 p.m. at 241 pounds. I will weigh in every night at the same time. It surprised me that I had had no Darvon since that last one on the road and had so little pain since. Well within the limits that I could handle. I am sure part of the reason was that I was so sure I would not hurt. Still, it was the first time in 42 years I was without pain relievers for that long a period of time . . . What a start!!!

I called home later that night; everything was fine. Well, I expected that. Before leaving for New York, I had explained to my family what I was going to do and that I wanted no worries of any kind during this period. They know how much this means to me and how I truly feel that this is my last hope. If this does not work, I am doomed to suffering for the rest of my life . . . I will have given up. If it would not work, what would I do? But that is negative thinking and I refuse to allow it to get hold of me. Anyway, my family agreed that unless there was a death in the family, they were to tell me everything was fine. Even though in our family business I do all the bookkeeping, they were to manage without me. If they could not manage, they would have to wait until I got home. Before I left, I did as much of the bookkeeping and advance bill paying as I could do ahead of time and left detailed instructions for everything. They were on their own, as I was.

July 31st, my second day at the Manor. Went right to sleep last night. Just closed my eyes with a contented feeling and right to sleep. Never did this before. Bed time was always a struggle, tossing and turning, sometimes for hours. Woke up about 1:00 a.m.

hurting. Not real bad, but enough to keep me awake. I did not take anything. I could not if I had wanted to. I only brought enough Darvon to hold me until I got to the Manor. I took my last one on the ride up here. I guess I just did not trust myself. The pain quit after a little while and I slept fine for the rest of the night and woke up in the morning refreshed.

For this second day, Ellie, Pearl and I made plans to go into town, but by noon, my pains started coming back and I felt nauseous and got real weak, so I stayed in my cottage to rest. The nausea passed in about an hour. The pain quit after several hours.

Talked to Dr. Gross about the pain. He said if it got real bad to ask for an orange. This would help, but to try not to take any medication. The pain is from the system flushing itself out and it will stop.

There was again a lecture at 8:00 p.m. by Dr. Lawrence. A truly lovely young lady. She is a vegetarian and slim as a reed. A great inspiration for those of us who also want to lose weight. Everyone there gave a little background as to why they were there and what they hoped to accomplish. Some were there to quit smoking. One couple was from Holland. Yes, Europe. Someone in the husband's office told him about Pawling Health Manor and about quitting smoking, and they came over just for that.

Several were there to lose weight, large and small amounts. One girl was getting married in three weeks and felt she would like to lose at least ten pounds so she was there for a week. I wanted to lose weight, but that was secondary to the pain. One lady in her late seventies was there for her arthritis. She arrived two weeks ago so bad she could not walk. Now, she is getting around by herself and feeling great. She will be here four weeks, altogether, and fasting on water, alone, for the whole time. She said she had never been in such great health.

My pains tapered off till nighttime, and then it became the worst pain I have ever had. Found it hard to sleep during the night. It took all my will power and energy to concentrate on not quitting and to not ask Dr. Gross for a pain killer. Read some, walked some, although they had told us the first day that the more we rested, the faster we would get results. I could just not get a comfortable place to sit or lie down. All night it was a miserable time, alternating between sitting, standing and lying down with a cold towel on my head, asking myself, "Why am I putting up with this torture? Why do I not just quit and go back to taking pills?" But, somehow, I did not quit and the night did end.

Weds., August 1. I started the third day with my pains dropping off slightly. Dr. Gross came in at 9:30 a.m. to take my pulse. They take it twice a day to check our progress medically. I asked him again about the pain and he again advised patience. Along about noon, the pains stopped. Completely . . . . . I was surprised and very skeptical. Kept wondering when they would start up again. Weighed in last night at 236 pounds. Went to another lecture in the afternoon, given by Dr. Lawrence today. There were several people there to cure colitis.

Colitis seems to be something that is very easily helped by first fasting and then going on raw vegetables and fruits. One girl came here five weeks ago and fasted four weeks, and is now eating. I saw her tray being carried to her room. My, what lovely food. Large baked potatoes, large salads, and lots of fruits. When this girl got here, she was in horrible shape. All the symptoms of the last stages of colitis. And even though she lost a lot of weight she did not need to lose, she is doing fine and expects to go home in another week and a half.

One lady is here who is from an Embassy in Washington. She became curious about being a vegetarian when her eight-year-old son started to refuse to eat meat. At first, she was worried because of our so-called good diet in this country of lots of good, red meat. Then, as she started to study diet and nutrition and vegetarianism, she became convinced that, in this case, her son knew more than she did. She is here to fast for a week and learn new eating habits, and then going home to put the whole family on this healthful way to eat.

Rested until 1:30 p.m. Then, Pearl and I went into the nearest town. I bought something to knit. I was really tired and weak, felt I had no strength left, but I also had no pain left, either. I can handle being tired.

Started hurting in one leg about 3:30 p.m. Just could not seem to get comfortable. Just lay in bed, and read, and rested. Time goes so slowly. Took two cold showers, which relaxes me, but it is also necessary because this is almost a heat wave, and although we have fans, there is no air conditioning. Another thing I was glad about because I like to have all my doors and windows open in the summer.

We have no television in our cottage; what a blessing!!! Before coming here, I was dreading the thought that I would have to share my room with someone who wanted to play the TV or radio. But all three of us feel the same. None of us want it, either. Nor smoking. It is amazing, but none of us smoke, either. Although the rules here are no smoking on the premises, every now and then, we can smell some, someplace. Do not know who, but it seems foolish to pay money to come here and then cheat. I remind myself that when I do not hurt, it is because of nature healing me and not through the use of drugs, and that gives me hope.

Talking about the cost, it seems silly to even think that this time here is costly. Our stay here of one week at this time, August, 1979, is $210.00, which includes the lectures, the doctor's care, the room, with maid service, constant fresh ice water and access to Dr. Gross and Dr. Lawrence. Which is less than what a good motel charges. All the time I was taking Darvon, it cost me at least $500.00 a year, and that did not include the doctors. In the eleven years I have been taking Darvon, that amounts to $5,500.00 for pain relievers, only!!! WOW!!!

August 2, Thursday. My fourth day, I had weighed in at 232 pounds last night. Spent a somewhat more peaceful night and had a very lazy day. Sunshine all the time, so far. The resort has lovely grounds and many huge trees to sit under. We do tend to congregate and talk. Most women knit. I have only seen three men here, so far, but they tell me there are at least eight.

No pain today . . . . . Went to Hyde Park and saw the home of Franklin D. Roosevelt. What a mansion. I was so tired I could not do it justice. Pearl, on the other hand, was bursting with energy. Dr. Gross said this was not unusual. Weird to us, but he said not unusual. The first time Pearl fasted, she felt the same. Full of energy and had a real struggle not to jog, or walk, or go sightseeing more.

After telephoning home, I made the decision to go home Saturday. I live in a unique place. It is the top floor of a 33-floor office building, and so, I would be able to have complete privacy and could continue the fasting with no company or interruptions. I even made a deal with my husband to take the telephone off the hook when I am alone so I could continue having my rest. He also said I would not have to fix him any food for the week or do anything I did not want to do.

Great, huh? Maybe our deal will last past that week. Well, I can dream, can't I????

Pearl and I had a long talk with Dr. Lawrence. She is a vegetarian and slim, vibrant, and healthy. She thinks meat is bad and that the best diet is one rich in raw foods and no refined foods of any kind. We will be shown how to make attractive meals and still stay within these guidelines while we are at Pawlings.

In the evening, it rained a little. Talked to the lady in the next cottage, who is here to lose weight. She has been here three weeks and lost twenty-five pounds. No food, only water, feeling great. She also, as a side benefit, lost all desire to smoke. From a pack or more a day to no desire at all. Isn't that great?

August 3rd. Friday. My fifth day. Weighed 230 pounds last night. Everyone up at 8:00 a.m. for some reason. I had an orange for breakfast because I am going home. It surely tasted good. Such a clean, pure taste. Lunch was a few grapes, three plums, and a few black cherries. Only ate half; I just became completely full.

Only had slight knee pain today for a short time and then it was gone. Time is going faster now that I know I am going home.

Pearl, Kathy and I went to the nearby Vanderbilt estates to see their mansion. Great, breathtakingly beautiful, absolutely marvelous, fantastic. I had more energy and was able to go all over the estate and grounds.

Hot weather, again; took three long showers since we got back from the mansion, and rested. Had a lovely salad for dinner. Romaine lettuce, celery, shredded carrots, cauliflower, raw mushrooms with oil and lemon dressing and tomatoes. What a banquet. I could only eat half of it.

I weighed in at 228. I have lost thirteen pounds for the time I have been here. That was more than anyone here lost in the first week. Could be because I have so much to lose.

August 4th. Saturday. Big day; not only eating again, but I am going home!!!! Packed everything before going to the 10:30 a.m. lecture. This was given by Dr. Gross' wife, Joy. Now here is a perfect example of what we would all like to look like and the health we would all like to have. She has been a vegetarian for most of her life and has raised her five beautiful children that way. No overweight here, and such skin, such bright eyes, and such energy. Makes you tired to just see them. She looks at least twenty years younger than she is. You can read her story in her book listed in Chapter 9.

What a fantastic way of eating. She told about the way to combat monotony in cooking. I should actually say non-cooking. Most of the foods are raw. After the lecture and demonstration, we ate the food they showed us. Yogurt and fruit compote. Eggplant with tomato and cheese, out of this world . . . . . Salads of all kinds, fruits and a special pie with only good ingredients. About twenty-five people attended the lecture, which is about half of the people at the manor. The ones who are still fasting did not attend. They will have the same demonstration on the Saturday before they leave.

Everyone there was full of enthusiasm for this way of eating and determined not to revert to their old, bad eating habits when they returned home.

After the feast, Pearl drove me to the nearest town where I was catching the airport bus back to New York. On the trip home, I thought I was a victim of the time machine. I hurt and hurt. The pain was intense. I thought it could be from the long ride and being unable to move around. It was the worst pain I had ever suffered. The absolutely worst day of my life. I was so bad that the airport people found me a place to lie down until the airplane left. On looking back, I wonder how I made it home. I had no pain reliever, just aspirin I bought at the airport, which did no good at all. I just paced the floor and lay down and then paced the floor and lay down. When I finally got on the plane and had to sit still until we arrived in Detroit, I repeated all the positive thoughts I could think of and concentrated on getting home. I do not know how to put this strongly enough. It was horrible. I found out later from Dr. Jourdikian that it was the reaction of being detoxified and adding that food all at once.

Sunday, August 5th. Slept late. A person's bed is surely the most comforting thing in the world. Well, maybe the second most comforting thing in the world. Being back with your loving husband is the first. Took a short ride in the afternoon with my husband, then he dropped me off home, and he went to eat. Remember the deal he made with me? I am going to fast for one more week and I do not want to be tempted, so there is no food in the house except his skim milk, and I would not drink that if I were starving.

Monday, August 6th. Although I hurt some until quite late last night, I took no pills. Had weighed in at 226 pounds. Felt like I had the Monday blues. I felt so tired. No ambition. Just a feeling of needing a complete rest and no desire to accomplish anything. I had read that some people experience a high on fasting. The Indian people would fast to achieve visions. My feeling was as if everything in life were rosy and perfect. I kept having the feeling that from now on, life would have a truer, deeper meaning and I would be more in tune with others and their hopes and feelings. I knew life was not easy and would not be in the future, but I felt as if it would be. It is hard to explain, but it is there and although it will go away, to some degree, I know I will be a better person for having this experience.

August 7th. Tuesday. Had my only company. My kids came over with a lovely bouquet of red roses, my favorite flower, and a lovely card full of love and encouragement. They stayed only a few minutes; their only thought was to help me with this fast and to hope my arthritis was gone for good.

I rested some and worked in my home office. Part of the deal was to allow me to take the telephone off the hook so I did not have lots of interruptions, because in our business, our telephone rings constantly. I did get some office work done. The more the mind is at peace, the better the fast. The day seemed to go slowly, and then, all of a sudden, it was nighttime. Fasting is restful. It is important for the person who wants to fast to have no fear of fasting. It does no harm and a great deal of good.

August 9th. Wednesday. Had two aspirin late last night. Just could not sleep. I do not seem to want to sleep as much as I did. I really felt in the past I needed nine hours, but I am sure in the future I will need less. My fingers are bonier, not all puffed up like they were or all swollen. My wrists hurt for a short time last night, but not during the day. What a difference in the pain. I used to hurt 40 hours a day.

August 10th. Weighed in at 225. Slept late; stayed home so far this week, but this afternoon took a short ride with my husband. Still no food. I only drink when thirsty. This is important, not to feel you should drink lots of water to flush out your system. Only drink when thirsty; this way you will not put extra strain on your kidneys.

August 11th. Weighed in at 223. No pain today, just tired. I feel weak, and find it hard to concentrate. It seems as if I can not zero in on anything. I just want to relax and enjoy life. There is no urgency and the feeling is that everything will be fine.

August 12th. Went to a business meeting in the morning. No problems there. Did find out that one of our managers skipped town the very day I left for New York, but because of our agreement, no one told me. This created a major problem, since the kids had to move into the building and run it until we found a new manager. But they wanted me to have every chance to make this program work, so they did not tell me. Rested the rest of the day and took no pain pills. Other than the aspirin on Wednesday, I have had no medication. When I count what I took prior to going on this fast, I am amazed. I never took less than 12 Darvon daily, ever. Sometimes more, plus a few aspirin, here and there.

August 13th. For my Sunday breakfast, I broke my fast with a large piece of muskmelon. Weighed in at 221. Had two oranges for lunch. Later in the day, I had some white grapes, but was really quite full. A little pain late in the day. Took two aspirin.

August 14th. No change in weight. Had a little

more pep. My husband took me to a new health food restaurant called Healthy Jones. We split their super special salad. This had everything in it. Sprouts, mushrooms, onions, cucumbers, carrots, broccoli, cauliflower, romaine lettuce, radishes and herb dressing. Delicious. Could not finish my portion.

This is a great place to eat if you want to eat nutritionally and deliciously. They have the best of everything.

I was still educating myself. I had many books on vitamins and studied very carefully. The more I studied, the more I found I had to study. Vitamin therapy is very individual. I understand now why doctors say, "You do not need vitamins if you eat a normal, nutritious diet." They mean that if we grew our own food without pesticides and with natural fertilizer, ate only meat that had no additives, ate only fertile eggs, whole raw milk and cheese, let no one else handle these foods and made sure that they were grown only in good, nutritious soil, we would not need vitamins. And they are right. But where can we do that? Whom do you know that can eat this way? The growing number of people who are studying and who do spend the time are doing so even though it takes many hours and careful shopping to provide their family with the proper foods. I will, in the future, find as many foods as possible.

Research shows that in peoples of rural areas, in primitive conditions, in remote parts of the world, who do just that are healthy. Heart attacks are virtually unknown. Arthritis is unknown. People work right up to their deaths at ages past 90 and 100. They eat no refined foods of any kind and get a great deal of exercise. This is what I am trying to do for myself and my family. But it is an uphill struggle. I am winning and I will win. So far, I have myself, two of my children who are doing it wholeheartedly, one child half-heartedly, and I am still working on the other members of my family.

From now on, my diet will be fruits, salads, lean meat, such as chicken, turkey, fish, vegetables, cheese. No junk food. See books in Chapter 9 for more directions. I will go into what I eat in another chapter. I will continue to study the subject so I know why and what for. I recommend that if you really care about your health and that of your family, you will do the same.

Started taking vitamins today; did not take any while fasting. The body is supposed to be completely free of anything other than water so it can go on about its business. The people at the Pawling Health Manor feel that with dedicated shopping and eating the proper food, there is no need for added vitamins and minerals. There is disagreement of experts in this field, so it is up to you to read and determine what is right in your particular case. I feel I have been undernourished for more than a decade and I need this help for awhile.

The desire to rid yourself of whatever health problem you have must come from within and not from the desire of someone else. It will only work if you are determined to have self-interest and do it for yourself. Do not confuse this with selfish interest. This is self-interest. That is why I am so pleased with my two children who are following the method. I gave them the road map and it was up to them to follow or not. If they still lived with us, it might be different; then I could control what they ate, but when our children live away from home, it is entirely up to them.

If I am not diligent, I know I will let one food slip in, and then another, and soon be back on the same unhealthful road I was on. I pledge to myself this will not happen. If I live this way, I will be able to go swimming with my great grandchildren.

This program is not easy, but when you realize you can go from hurting constantly to only a twinge once in a while, and the only change you made was in your choice of foods, then you know the right road. My joints are supple and I can move around like a kid again.

Pawling Health Manor taught me two slogans, which I have tatooed on my brain.

"A LONG SHELF LIFE FOR THE PRODUCT MEANS A SHORT LIFE FOR ME."

"IF IT CAN SPOIL, EAT IT. IF IT CAN NOT SPOIL, DO NOT EAT IT."

I read labels, now, and buy almost no food in cans. No food already prepared. My husband and I eat out a lot and this is a hard part. I still have cravings for all the junk food, and when I see it, I want it.

I hope this craving will disappear. If it doesn't, I will continue to eat healthful food and continue pain-free.

The following chapters will be your guide. Only your guide. Sort of a small path you can walk to find out more and more so you can hurt less and less.

I HAVE NEVER FELT BETTER IN MY LIFE.

"We should not let authority be truth, but let truth be our authority."

Chapter 3

HOW TO BREAK OLD HABITS AND GET WELL

I think this is the hardest part. We who have arthritis tend to compensate for our pain in our movements, habits and our day-to-day living. We even tend to use the fact that we have arthritis as an excuse not to do things that we just do not want to do.

It takes strong will power to change eating habits. I still have trouble with wanting the wrong foods because, inside me, a little voice says, "You deserve this sweet because you hurt, or because you are depressed, or whatever." After all, this little voice says, "The world does not know or care how much you hurt, so reward yourself with this food." And always the wrong food.

In the past, when I really hurt at night and could not sleep, and I had had all the Darvon I dared to take, my little voice would say, "Go on, you deserve some food for being so brave." I would get up and eat something fattening and feel better. I am sure I felt better only in my head, but the food went to my body and did more damage, and my arthritis got worse, and it was another vicious cycle.

We need a substitute for will power, and reading this book, and others like it, will make it easier.

WE MUST AVOID ADDING TOXIC SUBSTANCES INTO OUR BODIES. It is not easy to not have that coffee break or tea break or coke break.

Many of us are dependent on it. We think we need that lift. But it must be overcome for you to become pain-free.

It is not easy for many of us to resist soda pop or danish or cake or ice cream, but it must be overcome for you to become pain-free.

You might feel, if you have to give up all that, then why is life worth living? But it is. It is the end of hurting, and hurting, and feeling there is nowhere to go and no help available.

Cigarette smokers who finally break the habit are ecstatic about how great they feel. You will feel this way, too.

HOW TO REPROGRAM YOUR INNER SELF

Anything we do without effort, we do because, in the past, we have done that same thing over and over. Good or bad, it is a habit.

If you were to drink herb tea instead of coffee for several weeks, you would develop a taste for herb tea and you would have a new habit.

It takes time and practice, but there is a shorter way. You can condition yourself. By reaching your subconscious mind and changing the orders it now operates under.

It does not matter what kind of arthritis you have. The seven-day diet will banish heat and swelling and pain, if you stay with it.

For a great many, the diet with exercises will be enough. For others, you will need more time and effort, but do not give up. Contrary to some medical opinion, "YOU CAN CURE YOUR OWN ARTHRITIS."

Surely, if you know that others have done it, you can, too. And you can. I DID.

First thing is to learn how to relax your body and be quiet and relaxed.

1. Find a time every day when you may be by yourself in a room with no interruptions. Sit quietly; do not let stressful thoughts interfere.

2. Take short vacations. Take drives in the country, if possible.

3. Talk to someone who will listen; let off steam. People who talk things out with another have few health problems and better blood pressure.

4. Work off some anger or stress in a hobby or sport.

5. Stretch often. It not only feels good, but it helps us.

6. A warm, lazy bath is wonderful for relaxing.

7. Do not let minor irritations bother you. They are not worth the price you pay in poor health.

8. Take one thing at a time. Learn to put problems in a mental box. Do not think of any problem at any time except when you take it out of that box for that purpose. This way, you will think of one problem at a time.

9. Do not be afraid to be yourself, whatever that self is.

YOUR SUBCONSCIOUS

William James discovered, seventy-five years ago, the power of auto-suggestion.

The will obeys the thought pattern or mental

images in your mind and operates as they command. There are those who do not want to take the trouble to develop self-command. You must not let this be you.

Auto-suggestion is a process of visualizing how you wish to behave in certain situations. It is a picture-making activity in your mind of the fulfillment of desires.

To make your wishes come true, the wishes must be motivated by strong emotions. This is how to do it.

Sit in a comfortable chair, lean back and close your eyes for a few minutes. As you do this, let your emotions come forth until you have a picture of what you want. Picture it happening. Live with this emotion every night with the same thoughts. Go back every night to the same picture. Accept no negative thoughts during this process. Meanwhile, tell no one else of what you're doing. They will find fault with this, and with you. Keep at it.

People who are successful at curing their arthritis use this method and let no one stop them, or tell them about negative stories from doctors, or stories of doctors who have said arthritis can not be helped. Information is coming forth by the bushels that there is a way to cure arthritis. You are reading of one such help. The books I have listed in Chapter 9 of this book tells you about more of them.

TEN STEPS TO HELP YOURSELF

1. Sit in a comfortable chair. Wiggle your toes and put your arms and legs in a comfortable place.

2. Take three deep breaths to let go of tension.

3. Put your right hand into a fist. Then let go and feel what limp is. Do the same with the left. Then your leg muscles and face.

4. Enjoy this limp feeling. Relax until you feel so quiet you are conscious of breathing.

5. As you take each deep breath, know that you are going deeper and deeper into a state of total limpness.

6. Quiet your mind. Let thoughts drift until your mind is a clean slate.

7. See yourself enjoying eating meals of fresh fruits, fresh green salads, fresh raw vegetables. Feel the texture and taste of the crisp alive flavors.

8. See yourself doing even better the next time you do this.

9. Tell yourself when you get up you will feel wonderful.

10. Count aloud, one, two, three and get up.

Learn all you can about healthful foods. Read all the books you can find on nutrition. These may all be found at your library. I know most of these books that I have in Chapter 9 by heart. When I feel myself slipping, as we all do, I reread them and it gets me on the right track again.

Go to your health food stores and read labels. Your desire to stay well must be continuous. The method is simple, but doing it is hard. Put this saying up where you see it every day.

THE METHOD IS SIMPLE . . . . . BUT DOING IT IS HARD.

You need to remind yourself every time you are about to eat or buy food about the reasons why certain foods are bad and certain foods are good.

We are overcome with ads on food no matter where we look or what we listen to on radio or TV. Almost all these foods are bad for people, in general, but definitely for those with arthritis.

Genesis 1:29
And God said, behold, I have given you every herb bearing seed, which is upon the face of the earth and every tree on which is the fruit of a tree yielding seed, to you it shall be as meat.

Chapter 4
WHAT TO EAT .....
WHAT NOT TO EAT

If you can not do a complete fast, as I did, the following alternate plan will detoxify your system and give you a good start.

For the first 5 days, drink the following. Make fresh every morning one quart of distilled water, to which you add the juice of six freshly squeezed lemons, and enough honey to make it drinkable. Use no more than two or three tablespoons of honey. Sip this every half hour throughout the day. If you are a working person, take it to work in a thermos.

The next five days, just raw fruits, any kind, as long as they are fresh, not frozen, and make sure they are ripe. You can eat as much as you want. Stay on this for the full five days.

Then, for the next week, eat only fresh fruits and raw or lightly steamed vegetables. Also, add some vitamins for your problems, as explained below. After this week, the above will make up to 75% of your total diet. You will add small amounts of lean protein . . . This should be found in nuts from the health food store. Almonds are the best. Make sure they are unsulfured. Also get protein from your raw vegetables. Become a vege-tarian if you can or as close as possible. Dairy foods and meats are the culprits, stay away.

When I eat beef, my hands and ankles swell, so I avoid this. You will have to become a detective and search out the best foods for you.

After the fasting period, I added vitamins and minerals to my program. Later on, at the writing of this book, as I became more knowledgeable, I contacted Dr. Felor Jourdikian, who made a personalized program for me for my arthritis and for my obesity. She also made one for two of my grown children. At the moment, we are following Dr. Jourdikian's

program and are doing just great.

Here is the vitamin program I had made for myself. They were all natural vitamins, not synthetic vitamins.

Vitamin A	25,000 units
Vitamin E	400 units
Vitamin D	1,000 units
Vitamin C	2,000 mg
Calcium	200-500 mg
Panthenic acid	400 mg
B2 and B6	2 mg each

I took calcium and vitamin C every few hours if I started to feel any twinge of pain due to being a bad girl and eating the wrong foods.

Again, let me say, it takes personal study to determine what vitamins you need. Read about vitamins, try to find a doctor who treats with Orthomolecular method. See a source of such doctors in Chapter 9.

Do not expect to rebuild in a few weeks what has taken years to tear down. Occasional off days and upsets are to be expected, regardless of the food eaten. Patience and persistence are important. The right frame of mind and the determination that this is right for you, and you do not care what the rest of the family or friends do or say. You are responsible for yourself. If you become sick, it is no ones fault but yours. If others eat wrong, it is their responsibility.

Do not let anyone talk you out of it or make fun of you. It is your health, not theirs. They will say, "Oh, come on, it won't hurt to cheat just this once, it's a holiday, or whatever." Please do not let them do this to you. You are responsible for your actions and no one else. I just close my ears and continue to become healthier and healthier.

Do not eat any processed food of any kind. This eliminates "JUNK FOOD." None of the foods below.

White flour, or food made with white flour
Sugar, white or brown
Catsup (it is loaded with sugar)
All desserts
Jello
Any processed food
Pop, either regular or diet
White rice

Small amounts of butter, only, no margarine (it has additives). Choose your meat carefully; you might be allergic to beef or pork, as I am, or you might be allergic to fish. I am lucky. I am not allergic to other protein sources.

Some people, at first, will feel that this leaves little to eat, but they are wrong. It leaves lots to eat and all the right foods. This includes . . . . .

All salads
All lettuce, but mainly romaine
Peppers
Carrots
Tomatoes
Beets
Cauliflower
Green beans
All grains
Potatoes
Squash
Sweet potatoes
Celery
Cucumbers
Radishes
Onions
All vegetables in season

Either baked or steamed, never boiled, because you lose all the vitamins and nutrients into the water. You can purchase an inexpensive steamer to put in your pans at any household store.

Eat at least two salads daily, two helpings of steamed vegetables, brown rice, or potatoes. (They are not fattening.) Lentils or Chinese vegetables, grains and fruits. "My!!! What a feast."

All fruits are okay, but make sure they are ripe. In the ripe ones, the sugar content is different than when they are green. All processed foods are full of various kinds of additives. The U.S. Government allows 3,500 additives to be put in our foods. In Switzerland, they charge more for white bread than for brown because they want to encourage the eating of brown bread. They add no preservatives. We people with arthritis can not handle these additives. I doubt if anyone else can, either, but that is not the subject of this book.

The variations are endless and Chapter 6 presents some of my favorite menus. Use this as a guide only to prepare your own favorites.

Have you looked at the ingredients on a wrapper of chocolate? I will not name the brand, but this is what I found.

Chocolate, WHITE SUGAR, CORN SYRUP, milk powder, condensed milk cream powder, INVERT SUGAR, pectin, cocoa butter, DEXTROSE, cocao, corn starch, dried egg whites, SALT, BENZOATE OF SODA, lecithin, citric acid, sodium citrate, invertase, convetit, bicarbonate of soda, vanilla, gelatin, emulsified hydrogenated shortening, frozen egg whites, commercial imitation vanilla extract.

This vanilla extract is made out of vanilla coumarine, glycerine, white sugar alcohol, water, carmel to color.

Imitation peach-flavored ice cream is made of glycerine, acetic aldehyde, acetic ether, formic ether, amyl valerinate, benzaldehyde, alcohol water. UGH!!!

> *Chinese literature says,
> "Sickness enters through
> the mouth and
> catastrophe comes out of
> the body."*

Chapter 5
EXERCISES

Exercises are very important. I used to think that exercise was just to strengthen the body and maybe make you feel better, but would not directly affect your health. Now, I know better. Exercises help put oxygen into your body; the more oxygen in your body, the better the body is. For those with arthritis, oxygen is vital. It helps our circulation, and when this is properly functioning, we do not have arthritis. People with arthritis usually have bad circulation; their hands and feet are cold. When we do a minimum of exercises daily, we are half way to our goal. When we add the correct way of eating, we are home free, or I should say, pain-free.

I have gotten into the habit of doing the following exercises before I even get out of bed in the morning. They take about four to six minutes.

Lie flat. Raise both arms up and swing them, first to the left, and then to the right. Do this ten times. *Figure 1.*

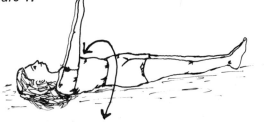

Figure 1

Lie flat, with hands by your side, and try to raise the upper part of your body as far as it will go. The first time, I did not raise it more than two inches and thought I would never raise it higher, but now, I can raise myself almost straight up. *Figure 2.*

Figure 2

Lie flat, with legs straight. Raise left leg straight up as far as you can. Lower it. Do this ten times. Then, do the same thing with the right leg. *Figure 3.*

Figure 3

Lie flat and raise both legs up together about 12 inches and swing them right to left in a figure eight. At first, you can barely do this, but it gets easier each time. Do it ten times. *Figure 4.*

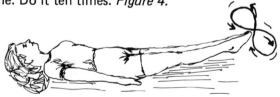

Figure 4

Lie on your left side and raise your right leg up as high as it will go; lower it. Do this ten times. Turn over on your right side and raise your left leg as far as it will go ten times. *Figure 5.*

Figure 5

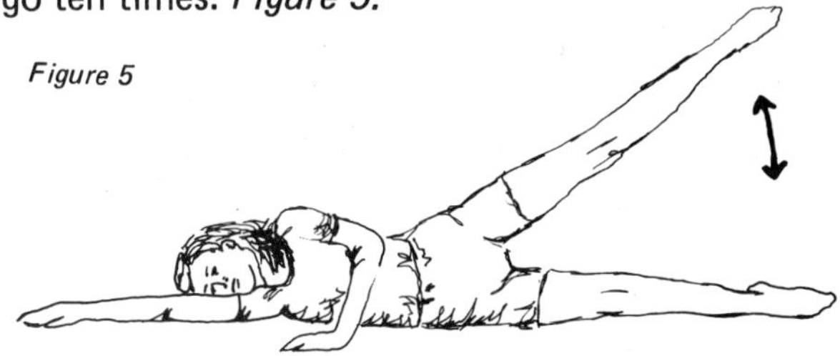

While lying on your right side, swing left leg over as far as it will go and back again. When you swing it back, make it go as far back as you can. Do this ten times, then turn on your left side and do it with your right leg ten times. *Figure 6.*

Figure 6

Now, you are ready to get up. Walk around briskly with as few clothes on as possible for up to ten minutes. As many times as you can while walking, raise up on your tippy toes and try to waddle like a duck. Swing your body around as much as you can. You will feel marvelous.

Now, I know some of you will find these very difficult. But *do* do as much as you can. If you can do only one kind, and only do that once, fine. The next day, add one more time. If you increase just one time every day, it will not be long before you are doing them all. As you eat properly, you will gradually find these easier and easier. I said I could cure my arthritis; I never said it was easy.

You will soon have a new view of life; I know. There was a time before I started on my quest of knowledge that I had to roll out of bed sideways because I could not get up any other way. Sometimes, my husband had to help me up.

There were days when I could only sit up for an hour and then had to lie down. We even bought a station wagon and had a piece of foam rubber cut to fit the back so I could get out for a ride. It had gotten so I just could not face going anywhere in the car because I could not sit up. In the past ten months, I have used this mattress about six times. And that was on a long trip when I felt the need to relax after driving for many hours. My husband would stretch out on it during his time off from driving. In the past, I did practically no driving. I am sure that the next car we get we will do without the mattress. Isn't that marvelous?????

Okay, now you have done your morning exercises. About noon, or so, take another ten minute walk. I do it in the house because we live way up in a building, and it is too difficult to go where I can walk. Besides, it is more convenient this way. I have measured off how many steps and how many round trips in my house make a mile, and I am up to two miles a day. The ideal time to exercise is for twenty minutes. By that time, your heart is really pumping and the oxygen is really doing its work.

When we travel, I stop at rest stops and do my walking. If I miss it, I feel sort of sluggish.

In the evening, just before bedtime, do another ten to twenty minutes of walking. When you start to feel better, you will find yourself adding these extra minutes without really thinking about it because you will want to walk more.

Here are some more very good exercises.

Stand straight; raise your arms in front of you together. On the count of one, pull them to your chest. On the count of two, spread them out as far as you can with a sort of bounce. On the count of three, bring them to your chest again, and, on the count of four, bring them to the starting position. Do this ten times. *Figures 7, 8, 9, 10 and 10a.*

Figure 7   Figure 8

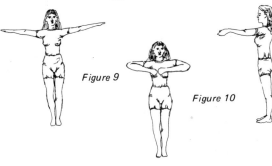

Figure 9   Figure 10

Figure 10a.

Stand straight. Raise your arms and make a circular motion like a windmill with both of them at the same time. Do this ten times. *Figure 11.*

Figure 11

Stand straight with hands at your sides and drop your left shoulder as far down as you can, then do this with your right shoulder. Do this ten times. *Figure 12.*

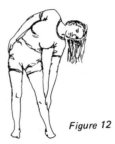

Figure 12

This is the only perfect exercise, and the hardest for those with arthritis to do.

Stand with your legs apart. Swing your right arm up and over your head counterclockwise across your body, then bend from the waist with knees stiff and touch, or try to touch, your left foot. Then whip your arm back overhead fast and hard and bend backwards from the

Figure 13

waist. This should be one continuous movement. Now, use the other arm. While doing this exercise, breathe in while changing sides, and exhaling while touching your toes. Do this until you can do each side ten times. (You will not do it the first time, and maybe not the 50th time, but you will go further down each time, and that is what counts. When your back becomes supple, you will easily touch your toes.) *Figure 13.*

Exercise for Improving Your Balance

Stand up on your toes, with your heels together, your eyes closed and your arms stretched forward at the shoulders. Stay in this position for 20 seconds without shifting your feet or opening your eyes. Do it ten times. I found this the hardest to do, and am still trying for the 20 seconds, but every day is better.

Strengthening Waist Muscles

Starting position: Sit on floor with legs straight out and both hands clasped behind neck. Twist the upper part of your body to the left as far as you can. Then, rotate to the right. Do this exercise ten times each side. *Figure 14.*

Figure 14

Strengthening the Back

Starting position: Lie flat on your back with your arms at your side. Take a big, deep breath and flatten the lower part of your back to the floor for five seconds, then relax. Repeat ten times, exhaling fully when you relax. *Figure 15.*

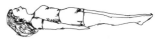

Figure 15

Exercise for the Kidneys

I do not have kidney problems, but this is one exercise that makes me feel good while I am doing it. Lie flat; raise both legs as close to your chest as you can. Place both arms around your legs

Figure 16

and, clasping tightly, roll from the right to the left at least ten times. My, but that feels good . . . *Figure 16.*

The Health Spas in Europe that have had excellent results with diet and exercise recommend a cold bath and rubdown with a coarse towel after exercising, or at least once a day. I have been unable to take a really cold shower, yet, but I am down to lukewarm. I also have a loofa cloth, which you can purchase anywhere in drugstores and department stores. I rub myself with that and it really makes my body tingle. I rub all over until my skin feels warm. I rub especially long in the areas where I used to hurt all the time.

Remember, we must have body motion, arthritics especially. It is increased circulation of the blood which helps nature to deliver nourishment to the body cells, including the unhealthy ones which cause arthritis.

The very fact we do not move much aggravates arthritis. So, we become progressively worse due to poor blood circulation. Mild exercise stimulates increased circulation to the weakened muscles.

Our blood must flow normally. It must bear food continually to build and rebuild healthy tissue.

When arthritics are told to exercise, they just do not. I know; I have been there. If your joints are swelling with heat and pain, hold off exercising until the diet works enough for the swelling to stop and then start these exercises slowly, but consistently, and add more each day.

Here are a few more you might like to add. While sitting in a chair, you can do these exercises. Move around while sitting. Move your hands and head, any part that you can do without strain.

Let your hands hang loose, then shake your hands. Do this several times a day. If you're in bed, do it one hand at a time over the edge of the bed. Remember, it is a start.

Sit on a table or high bench so your feet swing free. Stretch one leg forward, then let go and let it move as it will. Now, do the other leg. Do this three minutes daily, at first, and gradually increase to five minutes. These are not exercises, just body motion.

While lying on the flat of your back, point your toes inward. This takes effort to keep them pointing inward and up, but do it. Relax and do it again. Do this three or four minutes. Great for the back.

While lying on your back, raise your knees against your chest and pull your knees to your chest hard by the use of your arms. Relax and pull. Do this two or three minutes. You can feel this in the small of your back. As time goes on, you can increase this to ten minutes.

TAKE HEED OF THIS WARNING . . . . .

No exercise will be of any lasting effect if you do not change your diet to the fresh foods and vegetables noted elsewhere; in fact, they could harm you. So, unless you are serious about changing your eating habits, do not do these. You must also exercise every day. If we let more than a day go by, we have lost all the good that past exercises have done for us.

Walking . . . . . This is nature's perfect movement. It is the best there is. At first, a walk should be short, even if it is only a few feet. Make a record and every day increase it by 10%. Do this until you are walking for twenty minutes, twice a day.

Keep a positive attitude toward this and see how great it feels to increase the exercise.

SWIMMING

If you can find a place to swim regularly, do it. It is one of my greatest pleasures. Our bodies are weightless in the water, and the exercises which are hard to do out of water are easy to do in the water. Even if you are in a wheelchair, have someone help you into the pool and exercise for at least one-half hour.

This has been proven over and over, from polio victims to accident victims. Do not overdo it. I belong to a health spa, now, and the first thing I do when I get there is to go to the dry heat room for three minutes, then to the wet steam room for three minutes, and then into the pool to leisurely swim around and kick and enjoy. Then into the whirlpool for no more than three minutes. Then into the pool for several laps and into the whirlpool for three minutes, then swim for awhile, shower and go home. Before my change in diet, I would not even have gone, because it would just be too much effort and would hurt too much. Now, I leave invigorated.

Again, I remind you, the diet is the most important. YOU can get much better with just that, but if you want to truly be pain-free, you will have to do both.

Remember, if food has any additives, do not eat it. We who have arthritis or who have gotten rid of it cannot afford the so-called luxury of eating prepared food, chemicals, sugar, coffee or anything made with sugar or white flour.

You love to eat these fast foods, they taste so good and are easy to get, but what you are really enjoying is an indirect dose of stilbestrol, arsenic, or aureomycin.

We do not function well from these. They give us swelling and pain. So, every time we eat those foods, we know we are in for some pain, usually within three hours.

I used to reward myself for eating right for a few weeks by eating some chocolate candy or fried foods. Within hours, I had recurrences of pain and stiffness. After a day or two of proper eating, my pain and stiffness would disappear. Needless to say, you soon stop being so stupid.

No more. It is not worth it. I hope you will feel this way, too, and if you do, you will have a pain-free life.

Again, I repeat, as I do several times in this book, I can get rid of my pain by the foods I eat and I can cause my arthritis again by eating the wrong foods. Doctors have done this over and over with animals in laboratories. If this is so, and it is, all we have to do to never have arthritis again is to refrain from the foods we know are bad for us and eat those that are good for us.

RIGHT? Right . . . . .

"In general, mankind, since the improvement of cookery, eats twice as much as nature requires."

Benjamin Franklin

Chapter 6
SOME OF MY FAVORITE RECIPES

In Chapter 9, I list a number of books to read. Among them are several hundred menus. They range from simple meals to gourmet dinners. My style of cooking is very plain. I have found that I seem to like a very small variety of foods. Again, I have to say, this is something we have to discover for ourselves. I am very happy with this limited range of foods and my husband seems to be contented. He never complains, well, almost never.

These menus are always for two.

Baked Chicken

One chicken
3 onions
3 tablespoons of fresh or dried parsley
Vegit seasoning, about 1 tablespoon

Clean and dry the chicken. Place on a large piece of foil. Add the onions after slicing them. Sprinkle the parsley over the chicken. Add the vegit. Wrap tightly and put in the oven at 350 degrees for 50 minutes.

It always turns out juicy, tender, and simply delicious. For a real easy company meal, add baking potatoes the same time you put in the chicken and your meal will be done at the same time.

With the addition of a nice steamed dish of green beans, you have a scrumptious meal. Or, instead of a vegetable, you may make a nice salad. This is a meal fit for a King.

Potatoe and Onion Dish

4 potatoes
10 onions
Parsley, three tablespoons
Vegit, two tablespoons

Wash and slice potatoes, slice up onions into a very heavy pan with about 1 cup of water. Add the parsley and seasoning and cook for about 15 minutes.

The amount varies as to whether you want this dish quite juicy, as I do, or drier. Simply great dish, and so simple.

Sweet Potatoes, Onions, Carrots

2 large sweet potatoes (yams)
3 onions
2 carrots
Parsley, two tablespoons
Vegit, two tablespoons

Wash and peel sweet potatoes, cut in small pieces. Slice onions and scrub carrots. Do not peel the carrots, just slice them. Put all this into a heavy pan, add 1 cup of water and cook about 10 minutes.

You may add the parsley either before or after cooking. You may use either fresh or dried parsley in any of my recipes.

Acorn Squash

2 squash

Wash and cut in half. Clean out the center and place cut side down on foil in oven and bake about 50 minutes. To eat, just scoop out the inside and serve. I do not add anything.

For a complete meal, I put two baking potatoes in at the same time, make a simple salad and there, again, is a simple, yet nutritious meal. Suitable for your family or for company.

Crook Neck Squash

One medium squash

This is very good, in fact, the best squash I have ever eaten. Just peel, dice in large pieces and steam for about 10 minutes. Then mash it, add a very small piece of butter and Vegit seasoning and serve.

Wild Rice

2 leeks
3 onions
3 carrots
Parsley
Vegit seasoning

Add the above ingredients to the rice as you are cooking it, about ten minutes before the rice is done. If you have a little of your baked chicken left, add this. If not, add a chicken boullion cube while cooking the rice. Season and serve.

Special Chicken

1 chicken
3 carrots
3 onions
Basil
2 pieces of celery
2 potatoes

Clean and dry the chicken and place on the large piece of foil. Add the carrots, onions, basil, celery, potatoes, and wrap tightly.

Bake at 350 degrees for 50 minutes. Make a large salad and your meal is done.

Eggplant Casserole

One small to medium eggplant
2 large tomatoes

Slice the eggplant, put cold pressed safflower oil in bottom of baking pan, coat both sides of eggplant in the oil and bake for 20 minutes at 350 degrees, turning once. Then add a slice of tomatoe to cover each piece of eggplant. Bake 10 minutes more. Brown under broiler and serve at once. Fantastic. Even people who do not like eggplant will like this dish.

Cold Drink for Summer

1 Banana
4 strawberries
¼ cup orange juice — if frozen, use three tablespoons
¼ cup skim milk
4 ice cubes

Using your blender, put all the above in, place cover on and blend. If you wish a stronger flavor, add more orange juice. It looks and tastes like a milkshake, but is healthful.

You may use any variations of fruits and make a new drink every day.

My Favorite Salad

Romaine lettuce
Iceburg lettuce
Green onions
Cucumbers
Tomatoes
Fresh mushrooms
Alfalfa sprouts
Avocado
Shredded carrots

Wash, clean and cut up into a very large bowl. Add Vegit seasoning and small amount of my favorite dressing. I make this our whole meal.

My Favorite Dressing

4 tablespoons cold pressed safflower oil
1 teaspoon fresh lemon juice
1 or 2 tablespoons Vegit
1 tablespoon honey
¼ or ½ teaspoon mint, crushed
Sprinkling of Italian mixed dry herbs

Put the honey in the glass first. Then add the lemon juice and stir until the honey is well mixed. Then add the oil, mix well, add the rest of the ingredients. The above is enough for two people eating one huge salad. If you want to make more and store in refrigerator, just triple the ingredients.

Vegetable Soup

Celery, tops and all
Carrots, do not peel
Onions
Green beans
Lima beans
Corn

Put two cups of water into a large pot. Cut up larger vegetables and add to the water. Add the rest as is. Blend six ripe tomatoes in your blender. Add to the above. When it comes to a boil, simmer for about 15 minutes. If you want thinner soup, add water. Add vegit seasoning to taste. I also like to add parsley to soup. Also, I have some lemon seasoning which is nice. Also, a few bay leaves, which you take out before serving.

Add a small salad to this meal and a few nuts for dessert and you have a well balanced meal.

Fish Chowder

1 pound scallops
4 tablespoons vegetable oil
2 large onions
4 stalks celery (tops and all)
1 1/2 quart water
1/2 green pepper
7 yams (sweet potatoes)
3 chicken boullion cubes
2 teaspoons vegit seasoning
2 tablespoons cornstarch

Saute the onion and celery in the oil, add to a large pot with the water, green pepper, boullion cubes and seasoning. Cook about 20 minutes. Add the scallops and cook another 10 minutes. Last, add the cornstarch (which you have mixed with cold water to make a smooth paste).

Fancy Vegetable Soup

1 large tomato
1 cup peas
4 onions, chopped
1½ cup lima beans
1 cup zucchini
2 cups diced potatoes
½ teaspoon vegit
1 garlic clove
8 cups water
1 bunch parsley
3 tablespoons safflower oil

Saute the onions and garlic in a little butter or safflower oil. Put the zucchini and vegit seasoning and one whole tomato in the blender, puree this and add to the sauteed onions, and cook about two minutes. Put the water into a large pot and add the lima beans, potatoes, and peas and parsley and cook until vegetables are almost done.

Broccoli Casserole

2 large bunches fresh broccoli
12 large mushrooms
1 large onion, minced
¼ cup safflower oil
½ lemon

Steam the broccoli until just tender. Cook the onion and oil in another pan until done. Remove from heat and add the juice from the onion and a little vegit seasoning. Put the broccoli spears in a baking pan. Put the mushrooms, which you have sliced, around the pan. Sprinkle the lemon and onion mixture over it. Bake in the oven at 350 degrees for 10 minutes or less.

Baked Salmon

Large piece of salmon, preferrably
   the last cut near the tail
3 onions
2 carrots
1 bunch parsley
Seasoning

Wash and dry the salmon. Rub with the seasoning, place in a regular brown paper bag. Add the sliced onions and carrots and cut up parsley. Fold bag tightly closed. Bake this in an oven at 350 degrees for about 10 minutes per pound. To serve, take out of oven and gently take out of bag and place on a platter and garnish with a little parsley.

If you don't like salmon, you will like it this way.

Almond Fish

½ cup almonds
3 carrots
2 celery
½ pound mushrooms
3 onions
1½ pounds codfish fillets
Vegit seasoning

Dice all the vegetables and mix together. Place half of them in the bottom of a baking dish. Add seasoning. Lay the fish on top. Then cover with the remaining vegetables. Sprinkle with the almonds and moisten with about a cup of boullion.

Cover and bake in 350 degree oven for about 30 minutes. Remove the cover the last 10 minutes. Serve with brown rice and a small salad.

Stewed Chicken

1 cut up chicken
2 cups of water
3 tablespoons vegetable oil
2 tablespoons cornstarch
Thyme and rosemary, a pinch
Sprinkle of oregano
5 small onions
2 cups mushrooms
2 carrots

Wash and dry the chicken and sprinkle with vegit. Brown the chicken lightly in a heavy pan with vegetable oil. Remove the chicken from the pan. Blend the cornstarch and seasonings in the pan, add the water, when it boils, add the chicken and the onions, and carrots. Cook on low for 20 minutes, add mushrooms and simmer for 10 more minutes.

Pineapple and Orange Sherbet

1 6-ounce can of frozen orange juice
1 6-ounce can of frozen pineapple juice
3½ cups cold water
2 tablespoons undiluted frozen apple
   juice concentrate, unfrozen
1 cup nonfat dry milk

Put all the above in a large mixing bowl and beat enough to blend everything thoroughly. Pour into ice cube trays and freeze 1 to 2 hours until half frozen.

Put this mixture into a large bowl and, with an electric mixer, beat it on low speed until the mixture is softened, then beat on high speed for 3 to 5 minutes until it is creamy, but not liquid. Pour into ice cube trays again and freeze until hard. Several hours.

I have now found something that will make your recovery even faster. It has given me more energy, sounder sleep, and more of a feeling of well being. It has also eliminated bruising which I would get every-time I so much as lightly bumped into something. This was caused by the many years of aspirin and drugs prior to finding a way not to have arthritis.

It also got rid of an ulcer that my husband had for most of his adult life and it did this in about two weeks from the day he started taking this marvelous product.

I refrained from naming products in prior editions of this book but I feel I owe it to my readers to tell you.

. . . . **Barley Green** . . . . .

What is Barley Green?

It is a powder produced from the juice of the young barley leaves containing a wealth of nutrients — vitamins, minerals, live enzymes, superoxide dismutase, chlorophyll, proteins, strong alkaline pH and other nutrients. It is blended with powdered brown rice, a rich source of vitamin B_1, B_2, nicotinic acid and linoleic acid.

What does it do?

It helps the body balance, cleanse and heal itself. A healthy body repels disease and enables one to enjoy life to its utmost.

Nutrients found in Barley Green:

Concentrated 30 times, Barley Green is nature's balance of 16 vitamins and 23 minerals, all of which are still in their raw, naturally chelated and ionized form.

I make no "healing claims" for Barley Green. It balances the body. It delivers potent levels of nutrition and live enzymes on the cellular level, which enhances energy. This also allows the immune system to attack disease, thus helping the body to heal itself.

For more information please send a self-addressed stamped envelope to address on back page or check with where you bought this book.

"The Art of Medicine consists of keeping the patient in a good mood while nature does the healing."

Voltaire

Chapter 7
CASE HISTORIES

TWO VERY PERSONAL TESTIMONIALS

I feel I am blessed as all mothers wish to be blessed. I have done something lasting for my children. At least for two of them, so far. This program not only cured me, but it cured my daughter and my 29-year-old son, both of whom had arthritis.

I started with Sue, first. For the past several years, she has commented on how her hands and feet were swollen and hurt. There were many days when she was unable to work because she could not hold anything in her hands. Her feet would hurt so in the morning she had trouble standing on them. It seemed as if every year it was getting worse and worse. It took me back to the years I had hurt and how unable my own mother had been in helping. I hated the thought of history repeating itself. But what could I do except tell her to take aspirin and bear with it? The same as I had been told for forty-two years.

That was before my trip to Pawling Health Manor. When I returned from my fasting experience and was helped so dramatically, I felt I should try it with her. She had been diagnosed as having arthritis by two doctors over the years. When she was 13, she had rheumatic fever. Not a really serious case and, very fortunately, it left her with no heart damage of any kind.

From the age of 18, or so, she started having the aches and pains and heat in her hands and knees a little and in her feet.

When I discussed trying to treat her with my method, she was at the point of trying anything. She was desperate. I explained the method and that she would get better if she changed her eating habits. Since she works in our business and has a very physical job, and it was not possible for her to go away to fast, I asked her to go on a five-day juice fast to help detoxify her, first. She was agreeable.

I put her on the five-day lemon juice fast described in Chapter 4. I went on it along with her, to keep her company and give her morale a boost.

The first day for her was fine. She was able to take her lemon juice to work with her and sip on it while working.

The second day, she started getting nervous and jittery. She was also not smoking for at least the duration of the fast, and that was causing part of the jitters.

The third day, she was absolutely miserable. We talked on the telephone a lot to keep her going and to explain that what she was feeling was normal. She was restless, jittery, touchy and not sleeping well. On the plus side, her hands had started to lose their puffiness. For the first time in years, she was able to get her rings off and on easily. Her pains had started to diminish.

The fourth day, she started to feel as if there was light at the end of the tunnel. She was not feeling any hunger. Her joints were limber and her feet did not swell any more.

By the fifth day, she was able to hold her toothbrush in the mornings, raise her hands up high to brush her hair. She could not do these things prior to this fast. We both continued on to the fruits and then the vegetables, as I have outlined in Chapter 4.

That was almost a year ago. She now hurts only when she eats the wrong foods, and then it attacks her within hours. She eats plenty of fruits, vegetables, salads, fish, cheese and eggs. She refrains from beef, white flour, sugar and all refined foods. Also, about three months ago, she went on a more complete nutrition and vitamin program under Dr. Jourdikian's supervision.

She is no longer swollen or in pain. She flits around as every young girl of 25 should. When she is careless and eats the wrong foods, she pays for it. She is careless less and less as time goes by, as I am. One day, she was with a group of friends and they ordered a corned beef sandwich. She knew she should not eat it, but said, "Oh, it won't hurt just this once." By morning, she was so stiff and hurt so that she could not work. All symptoms left after a day and she says never again.

Can you imagine the pleasure it gives me to talk to her and hear she does not hurt any more? Can you imagine the anguish I used to feel when I knew she hurt and felt that my little girl was going to have to go through the years as I had and suffer as I had? But now, because of my showing her the road and through her efforts, she does not have to ever hurt again. My, how unhappy my mother must have been when I hurt, knowing she was unable to help me. I know she would have liked to do for me what I have done for my daughter.

Mike is my second son and had rheumatic fever at the age of 11. He woke up one morning burning up. His body was so sensitive we could not touch him. As the day went on, he became more and more sensitive. By the time the doctor arrived, he was unable to stand the touch of a blanket on his skin. The doctor who came to the house very gently carried him to his car for the drive to the hospital. He was given test after test. He had so many shots he was like a pincushion. One day, I asked how many shots so far, and he said he quit counting after 54. He became somewhat better, at least it did not hurt to have the sheets touch him.

On the 29th day, I still had no answer as to what they were going to do for him. I told the doctor that my insurance would run out on the 30th day. When I went to visit the next day, the release papers had been signed by the doctor and I took him home. He spent the next two months home, first being carried around by his brothers, and then gradually getting on his feet and back to school. Later tests confirmed he had no heart damage.

His arthritis started at age 17 when he was in a bad car accident. He recovered from the effects of the accident. It was a miracle the doctors said. The accident was on a Friday night. By Saturday afternoon, the doctor said he would probably not make it due to internal bleeding, and we should send for his brother who was serving as a Green Beret in Thailand. The Red Cross made the necessary calls and we began praying. So did the nurses and our friends. By Sunday night, he was taken out of intensive care, and by Monday night, when his brother Tom arrived from Thailand and walked into his room, he was sitting up. The doctors just shook their heads when I asked what happened. They said it was the will to live and prayers, because they had no hope for him. I like to think that by spending hours Friday night holding his head and talking to him, even though he was unconscious, and telling him over and over, "Mike, you can make it, try, try," that he heard me and did try and he did succeed. This plus the prayers.

He recovered from the effects of the accident, but several months later started saying his hands hurt. Later on, it also hurt in his knees and then in his legs, especially at night. Sounded just like what I had. It would not slow him down, though. He continued being very active in sports and working on a dude ranch after school and weekends. But the pain continued to plague him.

©

After Sue had such great success, he changed his diet completely. No beef, just chicken, turkey and fish. No refined foods, but plenty of fruits and vegetables. He and a group of friends go to the farmers' market every Saturday morning to buy fresh fruits and vegetables. They get large amounts and divide them up.

He was also put on a nutrition and vitamin plan by Dr. Jourdikian about four months ago. He says he has never felt better. No pain, unless he cheats, more energy and well being than ever. He is slim and vibrant and cannot sing the praises of the new way of living enough. He vows he will follow it the rest of his life and he feels it will be of great benefit in his new hobby of arm wrestling. He is being taught this sport by a friend of his, Cheri Fiebig. She is the undefeated world champion woman arm wrestler. She also did the illustrations for this book. She is only 19, watches very carefully what she eats. No pop, refined foods or sugar. She is healthy, vibrant and full of life.

MORE CASE HISTORIES

Dr. Jonathan V. Wright, in his book, "Dr. Wright's Book of Nutritional Therapy," Chapter 21, pages 189-196, tells the story of a young woman whose arthritis was so bad she could not even pick up her own baby, and all doctors could tell her was to take "aspirin".

Dr. Wright found that her arthritis was due to allergy to beef and wheat, and due to lack of digestive enzymes. She was also sensitive to potatoes, chicken, cheese and lettuce.

After her nutrition program, her arthritis was cured, but in her case, as in others, her arthritis would return if she ate the foods she was allergic to.

Dr. Wright, in the same book, Chapter 6, pages 231-235, tells the story of a man whose arthritis was due to sensitivity to the nightshade family of foods, such as tomatoes, potatoes, green pepper, eggplant. After he eliminated the nightshade foods, his arthritis was cured.

In "The Arthritics Cookbook" by Collin H. Dong, M.D., and Jane Banks, in Chapter 2, page 24, they tell of a young woman in her thirties who had been to five doctors and had been diagnosed rheumatoid arthritis.

She could hardly hold a piece of toast in her hand. After following the diet outlined by Dr. Dong, she has absolutely no pain, unless she eats the forbidden foods.

Another lady, eighty years old, came to his office in a wheelchair. After several months on the food plan he prescribes, she had lost 24 pounds and was walking everywhere.

In "THERE *IS* A CURE FOR *ARTHRITIS*," Paavo O. Airola, N.D., in Chapter 2, pages 88-89, tells about an Engineer who, at age 46, after being told he had liver trouble and jaundice and rheumatoid arthritis, started treatment at Bjorkagarde, Sweden. He could not bend his legs or arms, his joints were inflamed, swollen and stiff. He fasted 10 days, ate a special diet for 30 days, a new fast for 21 days. He stayed at the clinic eight months due to his damaged liver needing to be reactivated and rebuilt. All milk was eliminated and raw nuts and seeds used as a protein source.

He now leads a normal life, takes part in strenuous training and competitive sports. He has no more arthritis.

Paavo O. Airola also tells about a lady with five children who, before entering Brandels Clinic in Sweden, could not go upstairs, nor dress and undress herself. She was in terrible pain and helpless. After one week of fasting on vegetable broth and carrot juice, she felt much better and continued for 20 days. Five years after leaving the clinic, she is in her fifties and skiis, swims, takes long walks and faithfully follows her healthful diet. No sign of arthritis.

In the book "Bircher-Benner Nutrition Plan for Arthritis and Rheumatism," Chapter 2, page 23, the staff of the clinic describes the case of a 55-year-old teacher, still active, but with arthritis in the joints of her knees so badly that she could hardly get to school. She followed the diet plan at home and in a few weeks she recovered from the pain and stiffness. Ten years later, she is still cured, except for the brief times she strays from her diet, then a short period of proper eating and she is again free of pain.

In Chapter 2, pages 17-20, they also tell of a woman who was utterly helpless and bedridden. She was taken from a London Hospital to the Bircher-Benner Clinic in Switzerland. After several months, she was able to return home by train, much improved. Then the doctors in London decided to make a test with twelve patients, by diet alone, according to the Bircher-Benner methods. Beginning with two weeks of a raw diet, only, and followed by the gradual addition of whole cereals, steamed vegetables, potatoes steamed with their skins and vegetable boullion. All these cases were judged incurable by the doctors at the London hospital. The report on the results of this experiment may be found in the Proceedings of the Royal Society of Medicine, Vol. XXX, London, England. The results were, as follows: seven complete and three partial recovery of mobility, and two, no improvement at all. All patients showed considerable improvement in their general condition at the end of the treatment.

In "Let's Get Well," by Adelle Davis, Chapter 10, page 106, she tells of Mrs. C. whose hands were too gnarled to play the piano she loved so much. Following the change in diet, she was soon playing several hours daily in her seventies and continued until her death.

In the same chapter, she also tells of Mr. G. At 65, decades of pain had misshaped his tortured body until his chin was level with his knees. Yet, six weeks later, he was standing erect and working with hoe and shovel. All the result of changing his diet.

In "A DOCTOR'S *PROVEN* NEW HOME CURE FOR *ARTHRITIS*," by Giraud W. Campbell, D.O., Chapter 1, pages 21-23, he tells about a grandmother at age 65. Suddenly, she began to have pains and stiffness in her arms and legs. Her family physician diagnosed it as arthritis. After treatments for one month, he sent her to an arthritis specialist. The specialist said it was not arthritis, but frozen shoulders and sent her back to her family doctor, who said he could not help her. An arthritic clinic said it was rheumatoid arthritis and there was no cure and no help. Finally, she got to Dr. Campbell, went on his diet on a Wednesday, and by the following Saturday, was able to go to his office on her own with no help. She now does what any other healthy woman does.

On page 23 of his book, Dr. Campbell tells of a veteran of World War II, who, shortly after discharge, had lower back pains and shooting pains down the backs of his legs. He spent four years as an out-patient at the Veteran's Hospital, seeing them twice a week. No relief, but he was diagnosed as having "Marie Strumpell's" disease, which is also known as Ankylosing spondylitis.

He then went to an arthritis specialist who treated him for nine years with medication and injections. It gradually grew worse. He became crippled, pain was intense day and night. His spine became fused solid.

At this point, he went to Dr. Campbell and was put on a diet. Within two weeks, pain decreased 50%. His spine was still bent forward in a semi-circle which was gradually straightened so he now no longer walks bent over. If he had had this simple treatment when he first got the disease, he would have been spared years of torment and not become deformed.

These are just a few case histories. I give the names of many books in Chapter 9. These books should be available in your Public Library.

Instead of eating as much as possible, eat as little as possible.
"16th Century
Lueges Carvori"

Chapter 8
WHAT IS ARTHRITIS?

Your desire to stay well must be continuous. You need to remind yourself, every time you plan to eat or do grocery shopping, about the reason why certain foods are bad and certain foods are good for you.

Foods labeled "enriched" means first denatured, then partially restored. That attractive color in food is to make us buy it and words like "quick and easy," "smooth," are really warnings to us that we should not eat it.

I believe that people are changing and going back to basic foods. Natural foods are making sense to those who study and learn.

Read labels; if they have chemicals added, do not buy them. Watch out for fatigue. It is always present when we have arthritis. It is one of the earliest symptoms. There are two other signs that are fairly constant. A check should be made to see if you are in this condition. If so, contact the best doctor for arthritis in your area and be sure and inform him that you have become knowledgeable in this field and that you will take an active part in your treatment. It is not fair to expect a doctor to heal you. He can guide you, but the journey is taken by you, not him.

One sign mentioned above is the lowering of the amount of hemoglobin or oxygen-carrying power of the blood, usually to around 70% when 100% is normal.

The other sign is high blood sedimentation rate.

These are signs only a doctor can check.

What is arthritis? The word arthritis comes from the Greek words "Arthron" and "Itis", which literally means joint inflammatory disease. However, it is not only joints but connective tissue throughout the body. Also, muscles and soft tissue of several organs can be involved in the inflammatory process.

Close to one hundred different conditions are classified under arthritis. All have common symptoms of aches and pains in the joints and connective tissue throughout the body.

Rheumatism is a word that is interchangeable with the word arthritis and is mostly used in European countries and by old school doctors. How arthritis inflammation starts is not well understood. Several causes have been ascribed, such as injury, infection, auto-immune diseases (body producing antibodies against itself), calcium and vitamin D deficiency. Inflammation itself causes further damage in the joints and tissues, making them stiff and making normal movement difficult.

The symptoms and some of the signs of arthritis can be classified under one of the five most common kinds.

The most common form is called degenerative or Osteo-arthritis. The cause of the disease is associated with malabsorbtion of calcium and vitamin D. Although it is more common in the elderly, young people are not immune to it and, most recently, statistics indicate that it is showing up even in babies of three and four months old.

In its severest form, pain might cause disability, even commiting the arthritic to a wheelchair. This form of arthritis, while labeled incurable by the conventional doctors, in reality, responds excellently to nutrition therapy. The books "Arthritics Cookbook" and "There Is a Cure for Arthritis" are listed in Chapter 9.

The erosion of the joint bones can be stopped or retarded by correcting calcium-manganese-vitamin D-metabolism of the body.

The most serious forms of arthritis are Rheumatoid arthritis and a disease closely related to Reumatoid arthritis, but affecting the organs, is Systemic Lupus Erythematosus. These two forms of arthritis can be very debilitating and conventional treatments require such undesirable drugs as cortisone. The patient with R.A. or Lupus can be helped by nutritional therapy. Dr. Airola gives several case studies of R.A. and their cures by nutritional therapy in his book "There Is a Cure for Arthritis."

In the "Practical Encyclopedia of Natural Healing," by Mark Bricklin, he tells about Betty Hull of Corpus Christi, Texas, who founded a nonprofit organization, LEANON, which publishes "Lupus Lifeline". She outlined her personal nutrition program which put her condition into remission and off drugs.

Gout, which is referred to in literature and books written hundreds of years ago as "The King's Disease" because it is purely a nutritional disease. Genetically predisposed individuals produce too much uric acid. Crystals of the sodium salt of this uric acid deposit themselves in the joints and the kidney tissue. The inflammatory process can cause permanent damage. The simplest way to prevent gouty attacks is to limit eating food that contains purine, such as sardines, boullion, meat extracts, organ meats, anchovies, mushrooms, asparagus, spinach, artichokes, peas and beans.

The Merck Manual says drugs are so effective in lowering the serum urate content rate that restriction of the purine content of the diet is unnecessary. Really!!! Do we want to continue eating bad foods and then take drugs or do we want to eat the right foods and not take drugs? Doctors lean towards drugs. I believe in proper foods and no drugs. What do you think?

Mark Bricklin, in "Natural Healing," tells about using cherries to do the trick. Ludwig W. Blau, Ph.D., says he had so much torment in his big toe he was confined to a wheelchair. One day, by accident, he ate a whole bowl of cherries and the next morning the pain in his foot was almost gone. He continued to eat six cherries every day and was soon out of the wheelchair. If he forgot to take the cherries, it only took a few days for the stabbing pain to return.

After writing this up in the medical journal, he revealed that at least twelve others had had the same results. Twenty years later, he continues to eat his cherries or drink cherry juice and he remains in good health.

Ankylosing spondylitis. A rarer kind of arthritis, Ankylosing spondylitis affects men more than women. Muscle stiffness can occur, but when all the joints of the spine are involved, a humpback might result. Conventional treatment is only symptomatic, which means aspirin or cortisone is given to the patient to relieve pain. According to John R. J. Sorneson, Ph.D., in "The Journal of International Academy of Metabology," Vol. I, No. 2, page 7, 1978, Ankylosing Spondylitis and other arthritis diseases have been cured by a special chelate copper preparation and 89% of 1,140 patients had been free of the disease for at least three years.

At the University of California at Berkeley, Dr. Francis Pottinger (see reference in Chapter 9) fed one group of cats cooked meat and cooked milk. The cats developed arthritis on this diet and died of it. The more the meat and the milk was cooked, the quicker they developed arthritis.

Another controlled group of cats was fed raw food

and never developed arthritis. Then, when this controlled group was eventually fed the cooked meat and cooked milk, they, too, developed arthritis.

When the heat, pain and swelling disappears within a few days after eating uncooked and unprocessed foods, you will not care why it happened; you will just be thankful that they disappeared.

There is no longer any excuse for this painful arthritis condition to exist. It can be done by you and you alone. But you will have to study and learn from this book and others. Your public library is filled with good books on the subject of nutrition therapy and arthritis. But you have to do it yourself. I repeat, it can be done if you want to. I decided a year ago that the coming year would be devoted to the study and cure of my arthritis. I was completely exhausted from the pain and from the mental anguish that it caused. I felt there must be a way to stop it, and there is, and this is it.

Isn't that a great picture? Right now, visualize yourself within two weeks bending, and stretching, and not hurting, and throwing away all those drugs. In some cases, it will take longer, but every day there will be improvement, and you will never be as bad off as when you started this program, unless you back slide.

You will be able to take a trip on just the money you save from drugs, alone.

Take Mrs. A.C., who, at 51, had severe arthritis in the left hip. She needed crutches to walk, but liked her sweets and coffee breaks. She hated salads, never ate raw fruit, just sweets. Her diet was cooked foods and canned fruits and plenty of donuts, coffee and sweets. She felt she could not break the habit, but the pain finally got too bad. After a few days trying the more healthful way of eating, she found the new diet of raw foods, fruits, salads, steamed vegetables, and broiled meats easy to fix and delicious. She is now healthy and pain-free.

WHY WASN'T THE DIET PUSHED BEFORE? WHERE WAS THE PUBLICITY?

It was, but it did not get the publicity it should. I am dedicated to seeing this change.

Dr. DeForest Jarvis, who revealed folk medicine practices in his book "Folk Medicine and Arthritis," and "Folk Medicine," pointed his finger at wheat foods, white flour, white sugar, pasteurized milk, muscle meats and citrus fruits as being the factors for some people in causing body deterioration.

In his book "There Is a Cure for Arthritis," Paavo A. Airola, N.D., says the high incidence of success in Swedish clinics is fasting. Processed foods never cross the door. After the fast, only fresh fruits, juices and salads are served.

Dale Alexander, author of "Arthritis and Common Sense," emphasized those foods that lubricate the joints — those foods rich in vitamin A, such as cod liver oil, apricots, liver, carrots. He, too, emphasizes the whole fruit rather than juice. Especially important is the avoidance of commercially squeezed juices. The difference between juice you buy and juice you squeeze yourself is that the commercial juice was squeezed with the rind and any chemicals on the rind went into the juice.

All these authors did what they could, as I am trying to do to help you cure your arthritis.

As a final word in this chapter, do your exercises and relaxing techniques, change your eating habits and educate yourself about the environment. This will convince you of the need to be discriminating in choices of food and drink and that will keep you healthy.

Chapter 9
BOOKS TO READ

All these books are available at the library. If by any chance they don't have them, write to the Publishers listed. If that fails, write to me and I will try to find them for you.

THERE IS A CURE FOR ARTHRITIS, by Paavo O. Airola, N.D.
>Published by Parker Publishing Co., Inc.
>West Nyack New York
>Published in 1968

A DOCTOR'S PROVEN NEW HOME CURE FOR ARTHRITIS, by Giraud W. Campbell, D.O.
>Published by Parker Publishing Co., Inc.
>West Nyack New York

NUTRITION AGAINST DISEASE, by Dr. Roger J. Williams
>Published by Bantam Books, Pitman Publishing Co., in 1971
>6 East 43rd St., New York, N.Y. 10017

ARTHRITIS AND FOLK MEDICINE, by D. C. Jarvis, M.D., in 1960
> Published by Fawcett Crest Books, a unit of CBS Publications

BIRCHER-BENNER NUTRITION PLAN FOR ARTHRITIS AND RHEUMATISM, by Staff of the world-famous Bircher-Benner Clinic, in 1972
> Published by Nash Publishing by Pyramid Publications
> 757 Third Ave., New York, N.Y. 10017

THE ARTHRITIS COOKBOOK, by Collen H. Dong, M.D., and Jane Banks
> Published by Bantam Books in 1973
> 666 Fifth Ave., New York, N.Y. 10019

YOU DON'T HAVE TO BE SICK, by Jack Dunn Trop and Fred Allen, in 1961
> Published by Natural Hygiene Press, Inc.
> 1920 Irving Park Road, Chicago, Ill. 60613

LET'S EAT RIGHT TO KEEP FIT, by Adelle Davis, in 1954
> Published by Signet Books by New American
> P.O. Box 999, Bergenfield, N.J. 07621

LET'S GET WELL, by Adelle Davis, in 1965
> Published by Signet Books by New American
> P.O. Box 999, Bergenfield, N.J. 07621

MAKE YOUR JUICER YOUR DRUGSTORE, by Dr. L. Newman, in 1970
> Publisher Benedict Lust Publication
> Box 404, New York, N.Y. 10016

30-DAY WAY TO BORN AGAIN BODY, by Joy Gross, in 1978
Published by American Book
Stratford Press
Saddle Brook, N.J.

TRIUMPH OVER DISEASE, by Jack Goldstein, D.P.M., in 1977
Arco Publishing Co., Inc.
219 Park Ave., South, New York, N.Y. 10003

For a list of nutrition-minded doctors, write:

ALACER CORPORATION
Buena Park, California 90622

Send them 50c for postage.

PAWLING HEALTH CENTER
Box 401
Hyde Park, New York 12538
1-914-889-4141

Send self-addressed large envelope to Margie Garrison, Box 2053, Southfield, Michigan 48037, for a list of spas and health resorts.

Some day we hope to be wise enough to get the vitamins that wild animals get by eating what they like.

Chapter 10
VITAMINS

What is a vitamin? We have all heard of vitamins. There is much controversy about whether we need to add them to our diet, or is it enough that we get all we need from our foods? Do we get enough from the foods we eat? Many experts say "no". Vitamins are food. That is the reason I only take vitamins made naturally, and not those made synthetically.

VITAMIN A

Vitamin A is fat-soluble. It is found in green and yellow fruits and vegetables, milk, milk products, fish liver oil, apricots (dried), liver, spinach and carrots.

The bones, eyes, hair, skin, soft tissue, and teeth are all affected by the lack of this vitamin.

It aids body tissue reparation and maintenance (resist infection), visual purple production (necessary for night vision).

The symptoms, if you are deficient, are allergies, appetite loss, blemishes, dry hair, fatigue, itching/burning eyes, loss of smell, night blindness, rough, dry skin, sinus trouble, soft tooth enamel, susceptibility to infections.

Vitamin A will help acne, alcoholism, allergies, arthritis, asthma, athlete's foot, bronchitis, colds, cystitics, diabetes, eczema, heart disease, hepatitis, migraine headaches, psoriasis, sinusitis, stress, tooth and gum disorders.

VITAMIN B1

Vitamin B1 is water-soluble. It is found in blackstrap molasses, brewer's yeast, brown rice, fish, meat, nuts, organ meats, poultry, and wheat germ. Also in peanuts, sunflower seeds and Brazil nuts.

Our appetite, blood building, carbohydrate metabolism, circulation, digestion (hydrochloric acid production), energy, growth, learning capacity, muscle tone, maintenance of intestines, stomach and heart, are all affected by this vitamin.

The symptoms, if you are deficient, are loss of appetite, digestive disturbances, fatigue, irritability, nervousness, numbness of hands and feet, pain and noise sensitivity, pains around your heart and shortness of breath.

VITAMIN B2

Vitamin B2 is water-soluble. It is found in blackstrap molasses, brewer's yeast, nuts, organ meats, whole grains, almonds, brussel sprouts and liver.

It affects our eyes, hair, nails, skin, soft body tissue. It aids in antibody and red blood cell formation, cell respiration, metabolism (carbohydrate, fat and protein).

The symptoms, if you are deficient, are cataracts, corner of mouth cracks and sores, dizziness, itching, burning eyes, poor digestion, retarded growth, red, sore tongue.

Vitamin B2 will help if you have acne, alcoholism, arthritis, baldness, cataracts, diabetes, diarrhea, indigestion and stress.

VITAMIN B6

Vitamin B6 is water-soluble. It is found in blackstrap molasses, brewer's yeast, green, leafy vegetables, meat, organ meats, wheat germ, whole grains, desiccated liver, prunes, brown rice and peas.

It aids in antibody formation, digestion (hydrochloric acid production), fat and protein utilization (weight control), maintains sodium/potassium balance (nerves).

The symptoms, if you are deficient, are acne, anemia, arthritis, convulsions in babies, depression, dizziness, hair loss, irritability, learning disabilities, and weakness.

Vitamin B6 will help atherosclerosis, baldness, cholesterol (high), cystitis, facial oiliness, hypoglycemia, mental retardation, muscular disorders, nervous disorders, nausea in pregnancy, overweight, post-operative nausea, stress and sun sensitivity.

VITAMIN B12

Vitamin B12 is water-soluble. It is found in cheese, fish, milk, milk products, organ meats, cottage cheese, liver, tuna fish, and eggs.

It aids in appetite, blood cell formation, cell longevity, healthy nervous system, metabolism (carbohydrate, fat and protein).

The symptoms, if you are deficient, are general weakness, nervousness, pernicious anemia, walking and speaking difficulties.

Vitamin B12 will help alcoholism, allergies, anemia, arthritis, bronchial asthma, bursitis, epilepsy, fatigue, hypoglycemia, insomnia, overweight, shingles, and stress.

BIOTIN

Biotin is water-soluble. It is found in legumes, whole grains, organ meats, brewer's yeast, lentil, mungbean sprouts, egg yolk, and liver.

It aids cell growth, fatty acid production, metabolism (carbohydrate, fat, protein), and vitamin B utilization.

The symptoms, if you are deficient, are depression, dry skin, fatigue, grayish skin color, insomnia, muscular pain, and poor appetite.

Biotin will help baldness, dermatitis, eczema and leg cramps.

CHOLINE

Choline is water-soluble. It is found in brewer's yeast, fish, legumes, organ meats, soybeans, wheatgerm, lecithin, liver, egg yolks and peanuts.

It aids in lecithin formation, liver and gall bladder regulation, metabolism (fats, cholesterol), and nerve transmission.

The symptoms, if you are deficient, are bleeding stomach ulcers, growth problems, heart problems, heart trouble, high blood pressure, impaired liver and kidney function and intolerance to fats.

Choline will help alcoholism, atherosclerosis, baldness, cholesterol (high), constipation, dizziness, ear noises, hardening of the arteries, headaches, heart trouble, high blood pressure, hypoglycemia and insomnia.

FOLIC ACID

Folic acid is water-soluble. It is found in green, leafy vegetables, milk, milk products, organ meats, oysters, salmon, whole grains, brewer's yeast, dates, spinach and tuna fish.

It aids in appetite, body growth, and reproduction, hydrochloric acid, protein metabolism, and red blood cell formation.

The symptoms, if you are deficient, are anemia, digestive disturbances, graying hair, and growth problems.

Folic acid will help alcoholism, anemia, atherosclerosis, baldness, diarrhea, fatigue, menstrual problems, mental illness, stomach ulcers, and stress.

INOSITOL

Inositol is water-soluble. It is found in blackstrap molasses, citrus fruits, brewer's yeast, meat, milk, nuts, vegetables, whole grains, lecithin, oranges, and peanuts.

It aids in artery hardening retardation, cholesterol reduction, hair growth, lecithin formation, and metabolism (fat and cholesterol).

The symptoms, if you are deficient, are cholesterol (high), constipation, eczema, eye abnormalities, and hair loss.

Inositol will help atherosclerosis, baldness, cholesterol (high), constipation, heart disease, and overweight.

NIACIN

Niacin is water-soluble. It is found in brewer's yeast, seafood, lean meats, milk, milk products, poultry, desiccated liver, rhubarb, and peanuts.

It aids in circulation, cholesterol level reduction, growth, hydrochloric acid production, metabolism (protein, fat, carbohydrate), and sex hormone production.

The symptoms, if you are deficient, are appetite loss, canker sores, depression, fatigue, halitosis, headaches, indigestion, insomnia, muscular weakness, nausea, nervous disorders, and skin eruptions.

Niacin will help acne, baldness, diarrhea, halitosis, high blood pressure, leg cramps, migraine headaches, poor circulation, stress, and tooth decay.

PANTOTHENIC ACID

Pantothenic acid is water-soluble. It is found in brewer's yeast, legumes, organ meats, salmon, wheat germ, whole grains, mushrooms, elderberries, and orange juice.

It aids in antibody formation, carbohydrate, fat, protein conversion (energy), growth stimulation, and vitamin utilization.

The symptoms, if you are deficient, are diarrhea, duodenal ulcers, eczema, hypoglycemia, intestinal disorders, kidney trouble, loss of hair, muscle cramps, premature aging, respiratory infections, restlessness, nerve problems, sore feet, and vomiting.

Pantothenic acid will help allergies, arthritis, baldness, cystitis, digestive disorders, hypoglycemia, tooth decay, and stress.

PARA AMINOBENZOIC ACID — PABA

PABA is water-soluble. It is found in blackstrap molasses, brewer's yeast, liver, organ meats and wheat germ.

It aids in antibody formation, carbohydrate, fat, protein conversion (energy), intestinal bacteria activity, and protein metabolism.

The symptoms, if you are deficient, are constipation, depression, digestive disorders, fatigue, gray hair, headaches, and irritability.

PABA will help baldness, graying hair, overactive thyroid gland, parasitic diseases, rheumatic fever, stress, and infertility. It shows externally by burns, dark skin spots, dry skin, sunburn, and wrinkles.

PANGRAMIC ACID — B15

Pangramic acid is water-soluble. It is found in brewer's yeast, brown rice, meat (rare), seeds (sunflower, sesame, pumpkin), whole grains, and organ meats.

The symptoms, if you are deficient, are heart disease, nervous and glandular disorders.

Pangramic acid helps alcoholism, asthma, artherosclerosis, cholesterol (high), emphysema, heart disease, headaches, insomnia, poor circulation, premature aging, rheumatism, and shortness of breath.

VITAMIN C — ASCORBIC ACID

Vitamin C is water-soluble. It is found in citrus fruits, cantalope, green peppers, broccoli, oranges, papaya, and strawberries.

The symptoms, if you are deficient, are anemia, bleeding gums, capillary wall ruptures, bruise easily, dental cavities, low infection resistance (colds), nosebleeds, and poor digestion.

Vitamin C helps alcoholism, allergies, atheroscienrosis, arthritis, baldness, cholesterol (high), colds, insect bites, overweight, prickly heat, sinusitis, stress, and tooth decay.

VITAMIN D

Vitamin D is fat-soluble. It is found in egg yolks, organ meats, bone meal, sunlight, milk, salmon, and tuna.

The symptoms, if you are deficient, are burning sensation (mouth and throat), diarrhea, insomnia, myopia, nervousness, poor metabolism, softening bones and teeth.

Vitamin D helps acne, alcoholism, allergies, arthritis, cystitis, eczema, psoriasis, and stress.

VITAMIN E

Vitamin E is fat-soluble. It is found in dark green vegetables, eggs, liver, organ meats, wheat germ, vegetable oils, desiccated liver, oatmeal, safflower oil, peanuts, tomatoes, and wheat germ oil.

The symptoms, if you are deficient, are dry, dull or falling hair, enlarged prostate gland, gastrointestinal disease, heart disease, impotency, miscarriages, muscular wasting, and sterility.

Vitamin E helps allergies, arthritis, atherosclerosis, baldness, cholesterol (high), crossed eyes, cystitis, diabetes, heart disease (coronary thrombosis, angina pectoris, rheumatic heart disease), mentrual problems, overweight, phlebitis, sinusitis, stress, thrombosis, and varicose veins.

Externally, helps burns, scars, warts, wrinkles and wounds.

VITAMIN F

Vitamin F is fat-soluble. It is found in vegetable oils (safflower, soy, corn), wheat germ and sunflower seeds.

The symptoms, if you are deficient, are acne, allergies, diarrhea, dry skin, dry, brittle hair, eczema, gallstones, nail problems, underweight, and varicose veins.

Vitamin F helps allergies, baldness, bronchial asthma, cholesterol (high), eczema, gallbladder problems or removal, heart disease, leg ulcers, psoriasis, rheumatoid arthritis, overweight, and underweight.

VITAMIN P – BIOFLAVONOIDS

Vitamin P is water-soluble. It is found in fruits (skin and pulps), apricots, cherries, grapes, grapefruits, lemons, and plums.

The symptoms, if you are deficient, are anemia, bleeding gums, capillary wall ruptures, bruise easily, dental cavities, low infection resistance (colds), nosebleeds, and poor digestion.

Vitamin P helps asthma, bleeding gums, colds, eczema, dizziness (caused by inner ear), hemorrhoids, high blood pressure, miscarriages, rheumatic fever, rheumatism, and ulcers.

MINERALS

CALCIUM

Calcium is found in milk, cheese, molasses, yogurt, bone meal, dolomite, almonds, and beef liver.

The symptoms, if you are deficient, are heart palpitations, insomnia, muscle cramps, nervousness, arm and leg numbness, and tooth decay.

Calcium helps arthritis, aging symptoms (backache, bone pain, finger tremors), foot and leg cramps, insomnia, menstrual cramps, menopause problems, nervousness, overweight, premenstrual tension, and rheumatism.

CHROMIUM

Chromium is found in brewer's yeast, clams, corn oil, whole grain cereals.

The symptoms, if you are deficient, are atherosclerosis, and glucose intolerance in diabetics.

Chromium helps diabetes and hypoglycemia.

COPPER

Copper is found in seafood, kelp tablets, and iodized salt.

The symptoms, if you are deficient, are general weakness, impaired respiration, and skin sores.

Copper helps anemia and baldness.

IODINE

Iodine is found in seafood, kelp tablets and iodized salt.

The symptoms, if you are deficient, are cold hands and feet, dry hair, irritability, nervousness, and obesity.

Iodine helps atherosclerosis, hair problems, goiter, and hyperthyroidism.

IRON

Iron is found in blackstrap molasses, eggs, fish, organ meats, poultry, wheat germ, desiccated liver, and shredded wheat.

The symptoms, if you are deficient, are breathing difficulties, brittle nails, iron deficiency anemia (pale skin, fatigue), and constipation.

Iron will help alcoholism, anemia, colitis, and menstrual problems.

MANGANESE

Manganese is found in bananas, bran cereals, celery, egg yolks, green, leafy vegetables, legumes, liver, nuts, pineapples, and whole grains.

The symptoms, if you are deficient, are atazia (muscle coordination failure), dizziness, ear noises, and loss of hearing.

Manganese will help allergies, asthma, diabetes, and fatigue.

MAGNESIUM

Magnesium is found in bran, honey, green vegetables, nuts, seafood, spinach, bone meal, kelp tablets, peanuts, and tuna.

The symptoms, if you are deficient, are confusion, easily aroused anger, nervousness, rapid pulse, and tremors.

Magnesium helps alcoholism, cholesterol (high), depression, heart conditions, kidney stones, nervousness, prostate troubles, sensitivity to noise, stomach acidity, tooth decay, and overweight.

PHOSPHORUS

Phosphorus is found in eggs, fish, grains, glandular meats, poultry, yellow cheese, and milk.

The symptoms, if you are deficient, are appetite loss, fatigue, irregular breathing, nervous disorders, overweight, and weight loss.

Phosphorus will help arthritis, stunted growth in children, stress, tooth and gum disorders.

POTASSIUM

Potassium is found in dates, figs, peaches, tomato juice, blackstrap molasses, peanuts, raisins, seafood, apricots, bananas, flounder, potatoes, and sunflower seeds.

The symptoms, if you are deficient, are acne, continuous thirst, dry skin, constipation, general weakness, insomnia, muscle damage, nervousness, slow, irregular heartbeat, and weak reflexes.

Potassium helps acne, alcoholism, allergies, burns, colic in infants, diabetes, high blood pressure, heart disease (angina pectoris, congestive heart failure, myocardial infarction).

SODIUM

Sodium is found in salt, milk, cheese, and seafood.

The symptoms, if you are deficient, are appetite

loss, intestinal gas, muscle shrinkage, vomiting, and weight loss.

Sodium helps dehydration, fever, and heat stroke.

SULPHUR

Sulphur is found in bran, cheese, clams, eggs, nuts, fish, and wheat germ.

The symptoms, if you are deficient, are not known.

Sulphur helps arthritis. Externally, helps skin disorders (eczema, dermatitis, psoriasis).

ZINC

Zinc is found in brewer's yeast, liver, seafood, soybeans, spinach, sunflower seeds, and mushrooms.

The symptoms, if you are deficient, are delayed sexual maturity, fatigue, loss of taste, poor appetite, prolonged wound healing, retarded growth, and sterility.

Zinc helps alcoholism, atherosclerosis, baldness, cirosis, diabetes, internal and external wounds, and injury healing, high cholesterol (eliminates deposits), and infertility.

NOTE: *For any treatment or diagnosis of illness, see your physician. The use of certain dietary supplements may result in allergic reactions in some individuals. This chapter is not intended to be diagnostic or prescriptive, and I accept no responsibility.*

Chapter 11
CONCLUSION

I would like to say a final word of thanks to all those who wrote the books that gave me hope in my "Quest for Knowledge."

To Dr. Jack Goldstein (D.P.M.), who wrote "TRIUMPH OVER DISEASE." This was the first book I read that started to open my eyes to another way. He lead me on my first step on my path to "Pain-Free Living."

To Pawling Health Manor, who opened my eyes wider and made my goal clearer. They provided the second step to show me that the way was easier than I had first thought. They showed me that I was not alone in wanting to use this method, and that there were others before me who had accomplished what I had set out to do.

To Dr. Felor Jourdikian, who guided me in the writing of this book . . . . . who gave me advice and direction and made the day to day journey not only easier but possible.

To the many authors who are listed in Chapter 9 . . . . . who did their part in clearing my path.

To GOD . . . . . who, in his wisdom, put on the earth the pure, healthful foods that are all our bodies need for healthful living and who gives us our spiritual food that is all we need for pure living.

October 27, 1986

To whom it may concern,

Margie Garrison's "I Cured Arthritis You Can Too" is a note -
worthy milestone in the field of alternative treatment modalities.

I agree with Margie that with proper nutrition, exercise and a
positive mental attitude, not only is it possible to cure arthritis
but also prevent it.

Her book is simply and clearly written with a number of helpful
illustrations.

I have used it in my practice and highly recommend it. The pathway
to health is up to each individual. By following Margie's technique,
you can be free of arthritis.

Sincerely,

Learie N. Yuille, M.D.

LNY/km

Subscribed and sworn to me before this 27ᵗ day of October, 19 86.

Notary Public, Macomb County

KATHLEEN M. MARUS
Notary Public, Macomb County, MI
My Commission Expires Dec. 3, 1988

CATALOGUE

BETTER BOOK SERIES

Paper	_____ $ 8.95	**BUILD YOUR OWN HOME:** *ILLUSTRATED*

Paper _____ $ 8.95 **BUILD YOUR OWN HOME:** *ILLUSTRATED*
A Guide for Subcontracting the Easy Way.
A System to Save Time and Money.
Advantages and Disadvantages for the Weekenders.

Paper _____ $8.95 **BUILDING CONSULTANT:** *ILLUSTRATED*
The Owner's Guide to Understanding Construction of His Home.
What You Should Know About Building Specifications.
Advantages and Disadvantages for the Home Buyer.

Paper _____ $ 8.95 **REAL ESTATE BY YOURSELF:** *ILLUSTRATED*
If you sell it fast, you sold it too cheap. What you should know
about selling property.

Cloth _____ $ 8.95 **RENT:** *ILLUSTRATED*
What Every Tenant and Landlord Must Know.
A Guide for House and Apartment Owners.

Paper _____ $ 6.00 **TRAVEL BY CHARTER**
What It's Like. Where It's At. When to Go.

Cloth _____ $ 8.95 **MARINE MUSINGS:** *ILLUSTRATED POETRY*
Verse of the Great lakes Seaports, Ships and Seaman.

Paper _____ $ 8.95 **JUNKING BE A JUNK MILLIONAIRE:** *ILLUSTRATED*
What is Junk? The Changing Nature of Junk.

Cloth _____ $14.95 **GINSENG:** *ILLUSTRATED*
Story, How to and History

Cloth _____ $ 6.00 **CECELIA'S GERBILS:** *ILLUSTRATED*
A Story for Boys and Girls. A Manual for Adults.

Cloth _____ $ 6.00 **PINKY:** *ILLUSTRATED*
A Child's Story About a Dog, a Cocker Spaniel.

Paper _____ $ 6.00 **FUZZY BEAR:** *ILLUSTRATED*
A Baby Bear Performing in a Russian Circus with a Problem
to Overcome.

Paper _____ $ 6.00 **BENJAMIN VISITS THE JUNGLE:** *ILLUSTRATED*
Poetically Describing Benjamin's Adventure of seeing the
African Jungle for the first time.

Paper _____ $ 8.95 **TOYS WOODEN:** *ILLUSTRATED*
Beautiful small unique toys, handcrafted with simple tools.

_____ **Total for Books**

_____ **Michigan Tax**

_____ **Postage**

_____ **TOTAL**

Mail To: **HOLLAND HOUSE PRESS**
P.O. Box 42
Northville, Michigan 48167
Telephone: 1-313-273-0223

Holland House

CHECK FOR _____ENCLOSED

NAME _____

ADDRESS _____

CITY & STATE _____ ZIP _____

Orders from individuals must be accompanied by payment. No C.O.D., please.
Discounts available for Libraries, Bookstores and Wholesalers.

The Health Library
BOOK LIST

NOTE: *Not all of our books are strictly Hygienic. However, all have merit.*

NATURAL HYGIENE BOOKS

Life Science **Basic Health Library** (15 volumes)............$20.00
(Individual Volumes as priced below)
Better Sleep for a Better Life.......................................$2.00
Correct Food Combining for Easy Digestion...................$1.75
FASTING: Fastest Way to Superb Health........................$2.00
Great Power Within You..$1.75
Great Water Controversy...$2.50
Happy Truth About Protein...$1.00
How and Where to Buy Foods Wholesale.......................$3.00
How to Overcome Ailments...$1.75
The Miracle of Living Foods..$2.00
The Myth of Medicine..$2.50
Program for Perfect Health...$1.75
Super Foods for Super Health.......................................$1.75
Toxemia Explained..$3.00
The Ultimate Diet...$1.75

DR. HERBERT M. SHELTON COLLECTION

Exercise...$2.25
Fasting Can Save Your Life...$4.50
Fasting for the Health of It...$8.95
Fasting for Renewal of Life..$3.25
Food Combining Made Easy..$4.45
Getting Well..$5.00
Guide to the Joyous Life..$2.75
Health for All...$5.00
Health for the Millions...$3.00
Human Life: Its Philosophies and Laws.........................$25.00
Hygienic Care of Children..$7.45
Hygienic System, Volume I...$7.50
Introduction to Natural Hygiene....................................$3.50
Living Life to Live it Longer..$4.00
The Science and Fine Art of Fasting...............................$8.00
Superior Nutrition..$5.25
Syphilis: Werewolf of Medicine.....................................$8.00

OTHER NATURAL HYGIENE BOOKS

Composition and Facts About Foods/Ford........................$7.50
The Cruel Hoax Called Herpes Genitalis/Fry, Hazard........$4.95
Drug Medicine/Trall..$6.50
Dynamic Health/T. C. Fry..$1.00
Fasting for Health and Long Life/Dr. Carrington...............$4.50
Food Combining Simplified/Nelson................................$1.50
Guidelines of Life (GOLDOT)/Lewis E. Cook..................$25.50
History of Natural Hygiene & Principles of Natural Hygiene/
    Carrington & Shelton..$3.50
Is Menstruation Necessary?/Harris & MacDonald.............$1.75
The Natural Food of Man/Hereward Carrington................$6.50
No Breakfast Plan/Dr. Dewey..$6.00
Overcoming Asthma/Beth Snodgrass..............................$3.00
Scientific Fasting/Dr. Hazzard.......................................$8.00
Triumph Over Disease by Fasting/Goldstein.....................$2.50
Vaccination Condemned/Elben.....................................$13.00
Vaccinations Do Not Protect/Elben................................$1.75

OTHER HEALTH BOOKS OF MERIT

Art of Seeing/Aldous Huxley...$6.95
Cancer: Total Approach/Paavo Airola, N.C......................$3.00

Confessions of a Medical Heretic/Mendelsohn.................$3.95
Disease and Its Causes/Ellen G. White............................$3.25
Fluoride: The Aging Factor/Yiamouyiannis.....................$11.95
Juice Fasting/Paavo Airola, N.C....................................$4.95
Male Practice—How Doctors Manipulate Women/Mendelsohn. $6.95
Miracle of Sprouting/Stephen Blauer..............................$4.95
Natural Foods for Folks Who Eat/Dick Gregory................$3.95
Raw Foodist Propaganda/Joe Alexander.........................$3.95
The Vegetarian Alternative/Vic Sussman.........................$8.95
What's Wrong With Eating Meat?...................................$2.25

GARDENING BOOKS

Basic Book of Organic Gardening, updated/revised...........$6.95
Bug Book: Harmless Insect Control/Philbrick...................$5.95
How to Grow More Vegetables/Jeavons NEW REVISED ED....$7.95

COOKBOOKS and OTHER BOOKS FOR THE KITCHEN

Beansprout Book (All About Sprouting)...........................$2.95
Cookless Recipe Book/Richter.......................................$2.25
Diet and Salad Suggestions/Dr. Walker...........................$4.95
Dry and Save...$4.95
Dry It-You'll Like It/How to Dry Fruits and Vegetables.......$4.95
Light Eating for Survival/Marcia Acciardo.......................$5.95
Live Foods: 192 Vegetarian Raw Foods/Fathman..............$2.75
Raw Fruits and Vegetables/Bircher-Benner......................$2.50
Recipes for Long Life/Dr. Ann Wigmore..........................$8.95
Ten Talents Cookbook/Hurd (A Great Book!)....................$9.95
Un-Cook Book—Raw Food Adventures to a New Health High/
    Baker..$5.95
Vegan Kitchen/Freya Dinshah.......................................$4.50

PREGNANCY AND NATURAL CHILD CARE

Creation of Life, Achieving or Avoiding Pregnancy/Guay.......$6.95
Hygienic Care of Children/Shelton.................................$7.45
New Age Child Care Book/Dr. Ann Wigmore...................$5.95
Nursing Your Baby/Karen Pryor.....................................$2.95
Special Delivery-Complete Guide to Informed Birth/Baldwin. .$10.75
Spiritual Midwifery/Ina May NEW REVISED, Enlarged Ed.....$10.00

CASSETTE TAPES

Dr. Herbert M. Shelton—Set of Four.............................$20.45
(individual tapes as priced below)
LS-1 The Master Drama of Life......................................$6.45
LS-2 Toxemia and Its Results...$6.45
LS-3 How to Get Well and How to Stay Well.....................$6.45
LS-4 Proper Foods and Their Preparation........................$6.45

OTHER HEALTH AIDS

Illustrated Full Color Food Combining Place Mat...............$5.45
Set of Six (6) Place Mats...$25.45
Food Combining Post Cards................................6 for $1.00
25 Food Combining Post Cards......................................$4.50
Food Combining Guide (Chart)......................................$9.95
Combine When You Dine Recipe Guide (Chart)..................$9.95
The Food Combining Pocket Guide.................................$1.95
Unique No Smoking Signs...................................4 for $0.50
....10 for $1.00
....100 for $8.00

TO: _____

_____

_____

_____

Forwarding and return postage guaranteed
BOOKS FOURTH CLASS
THIS IS YOUR SHIPPING LABEL

ORDER FORM

Fill out form completely. Print or type information. Return entire form.

NUMBER WANTED	BOOK TITLE	PRICE PER ITEM	TOTAL
		$	$
		$	$
		$	$
		$	$
		$	$
		$	$
		$	$
		$	$
		$	$
		$	$
		$	$
		$	$
		$	$
		$	$
		$	$
		$	$
		$	$
		$	$

Date_____

SUBTOTAL FOR ORDER		$
POSTAGE (We pay postage on orders over $25.)		$ 1.00
TEXAS RESIDENT ONLY 4% STATE SALES TAX		$
TOTAL DUE		$

KEY TO SYMBOLS

T/O	TEMPORARILY OUT · BACK ORDERED
REP	BEING RE·PRINTED BACK ORDERED
NYP	NOT YET PUBLISHED · BACK ORDERED
O/P	OUT·OF·PRINT CANCELLED
DNS	DO NOT STOCK CANCELLED
SUB	NEW FORM OF PUBLICATION SUBSTITUTED
DIS	DISCONTINUED

(   ) _____
Area Code   Telephone No.

46

LEONARD J. PORTNER, M.D. FAAFP

_____FAMILY PRACTICE_____STRESS REDUCTION_____PREVENTIVE MEDICINE_

Margie Garrison, has in <u>I Cured My Arthritis You Can Too,</u>
once again proven the adage that "we are what we eat" and
also has artfully shown that we are responsible for our own
bodies and that since we cause our ailments we obviously have
the power to cure ourself of these ailments.

Mrs. Garrison points out that we are programmed by our
physicians i.e. "you will get progressively worse" or
"there is nothing that can be done..you will be in a wheel
chair within five years". When we listen to our physicians
they are usually correct in their estimates and because they
have a track record of being correct we listen to them. Thus
the vicious cycle of placing physicians in an all knowing,
all powerful position is established. The key to the physicians
correct prediction is of course our belief in his/her words
and therefore our self programming to perform just as we are
supposed to. Margie Garrison breaks this cycle. She shows
how through proper nutrition, proper positive mental attitude and determination plus exercise she was able to cure
herself and two children and how many of us following her
lead will be able to cure ourselves of not only arthritis, but
other conditions as well. More importantly we can, by using these techniques, prevent these maladies from occuring
in the first place.

Medical science is beginning to understand and "prove" how
much nutrition works. We are learning about the anti-oxi-
dant properties of vitamin A,C,E and Selenium. We have
studies showing that many cancer growths in laboratories are
inhibited by the presence of these chemicals.

We also are learning about why diet helps arthritis. We now
know why many of the foods Margie puts on the NO LIST are
there. They contain chemicals that cause the body to produce
chemicals called Inflammatory Prostaglandins which are directly responsible for the flaring of certain arthritic conditions.

Margie has shown us a practical way to begin a journey. We
need only follow the path and say-- "Thank you, Margie."

Subscribed and sworn before me theis I9th
day of November appeared Margie Garrison

Dianne M. Shovely _Dianne Shovely_
Notary Public,Wayne County, Mich
Acting in _Wayne_ County, Mich
My commission expires May I6, I984   Leonard J. Portner

INDEX

Illustrations By

Geoffery
McGaffey

CMCG

NOTES

NOTES

NOTES

NOTES